Stephen C. McGuinn | Alan S. Bruce
Quinnipiac University

A RE-INTRODUCTION TO CRIMINAL JUSTICE

Kendall Hunt
publishing company

Cover image © Shutterstock.com

Kendall Hunt
publishing company

www.kendallhunt.com
Send all inquiries to:
4050 Westmark Drive
Dubuque, IA 52004-1840

ISBN: 978-1-5249-7727-6

Published in the United States of America

TABLE OF CONTENTS

CHAPTER 1
INTRODUCTION

> Two neighbors are talking about conditions in their neighborhood. The first neighbor, Allie, is upset because she keeps getting approached by a man on a bike who is homeless and is asking for money. Recently, this man approached her in her driveway.
>
> "I wish I had been carrying when he approached me today," Allie remarks later to her neighbor, Janet.
>
> "Oh, I know how you feel," Janet responds. "I always try to carry change with me wherever I go."

We don't all see the world the same way. We don't all see people in the same way. Understanding this is important. The above story is remarkable in illustrating that we often bring such different perspectives to a situation. Likewise, we hope our work offers something that other perspectives, and other texts, do not. We believe our work addresses weaknesses characteristic of introductory texts, weaknesses that conspire to produce students more likely to adopt existing prevailing beliefs and replicate existing practices than to fulfill their potential as innovators in the field, equipped to critically examine the complex issues of crime and justice, and reach interesting and (perhaps) unique solutions offering change for the better. To paraphrase Nell Bernstein from *Burning Down the House*, we believe existing texts often encourage students to "build a better mousetrap"; our approach is to consider *why* we have the mousetrap, *why* we continue to use the mousetrap, and *whether* there are alternatives to the mousetrap that might be more appropriate. Like Heffernen (2017) we believe criminal justice education is often "exclusively descriptive ... students are introduced to the causes of crime, the operation of law enforcement and correction agencies and the rules of adjudication followed by the legal system" (2017, p. 114). Such a descriptive approach discourages substantive questions fundamental to our discipline. For example, it is not enough to know how police departments are structured (although this is important); students must also be encouraged to ask *why* we have police and *what* do we want them to do if we are to develop insight into policing. To this end, we hope our text raises questions about criminal justice rather than providing what appear to be the "correct" answers.

A recent article by Sever and Grillo (2016) helps illustrate our approach. Sever and Grillo examined introductory criminal justice textbooks for evidence of images that reinforce existing stereotypes by analyzing pictures used in a sample of introductory texts. Their findings suggest introductory texts often reinforce stereotypes that may be harmful. For example, they note that images of police wrongdoing most often depict officers as White, while images of those who offend—although predominantly White—show a considerable increase in the proportion of non-Whites. Importantly, these authors discuss the utility of their findings:

> Is it really the duty of a criminal justice textbook to dismiss stereotypes of crime or instill stereotypes that may be favorable to building a more diverse criminal justice system? **If** a majority of the arrests for violent blue-collar crime consist of minorities, is it the responsibility of the textbook to question these arrests **by** presenting alternative images within the textbook, or do they have a responsibility to merely represent what occurs in society and refrain from using the textbook as a platform for

> change? Since the majority of police officers in the United States are still white males today, should textbook pictures be in line with these proportions, or should they perpetuate an image that is not the reality in the field? (72)

This is central to our approach, it is our contention that the introductory text should do more than "merely represent what occurs in society." While it is important to understand what happens in society, we believe effective criminal justice education informs students as to "what is happening" while encouraging them to think about "*why* it is happening." Without asking "why," we believe our students are doomed to continue existing practices and will lack the capacity to assess the need for a change in practice. If assessment suggests change is needed, then students must be able to analyze the issue and introduce changes that are most likely to produce desired outcomes. Often these changes require students to create an entirely new tool belt. Although a crude analogy, understanding how to apply leaches to cure illness does not encourage thinking about whether leaches actually cure illness.

We also believe existing texts fail to acknowledge the unique subject matter of criminal justice, and this failure is an obstacle to effective education. Let's say a student attends college to study physics. It is most likely she does so because at some point in her life she has become interested in the subject matter and wishes to learn more about it. It is also likely the basics of her discipline have been presented to her by a qualified physics teacher in an academic setting so when she attends college she has an accurate and credible knowledge base for her study. This is not so in criminal justice. While students may be attracted to the major because of interest in the field, how their interest has emerged is important, and we contend understanding how people develop their interest in crime is important for how they process information.

There are many sources of information about crime but a good deal of research demonstrates most information comes from mass media (Lambert, 2005) and that media-generated information is highly influential and misleading. The general public is largely misinformed about crime. For example, responses to the Gallup Poll question "Is there more crime in the US than there was a year ago, or less?" in every poll from 1989 to 2016 shows that those sampled believed there was an increase in the crime rate (http://www.gallup.com/poll/1603/crime.aspx), despite considerable variation and an overall decline since the mid-1990s. Research on student knowledge has also found that students who consume the most crime-related media hold more inaccurate views about the criminal justice system (Barthe et al., 2013). There is also evidence that preference for a particular type of crime-related content impacts career aspirations—in a study of students in Introduction to criminal justice classes at two universities. Barthe et al. (2013) found that students who prefer police shows are more likely to want to be police, while those who watch court shows seek legal careers. The researchers also reported that "respondents considered the influence of crime-related television shows to be the primary contributor to major selection, and generated a mean influence score over twice that of high school career counselors" (2013, p. 23).

Clearly then there is great difference in how students entering the fields of physics and criminal justice have been prepared. Physics students have most likely been informed about physics from a qualified teacher in an academic setting and likely have accurate information about the field. Criminal justice students have generally learned about their field from exposure to inaccurate and exaggerated material presented in an entertaining media format: while the physics student is educated about their subject, the criminal justice student is misled. To effectively educate students of criminal justice, instructors must raise awareness of existing beliefs among students and determine the formation and accuracy of those beliefs. The field of metacognition is useful in this pursuit. The field has established the importance of making students aware of how their beliefs have been formed. As described by Cundiff and Finchbaugh (2016):

> Metacognition is often described simply as "thinking about thinking," but it involves complex processes that hold the potential of a more dynamic and flexible understanding of one's self as a thinker and a learner. (2016, p. 1)

Ambrose et al. (2010) state that metacognition is vital for people to become self-directed learners as they must be able to "assess the demands of the task, evaluate their own knowledge and skills, plan their approach, monitor their progress, and adjust their strategies as needed" (2010, p. 191). Another crucial difference between the fields of physics and criminal justice is the nature of the subject matter. Crime-related issues often bring to life emotions and beliefs that do not arise in the study of physics. For example, the criminal justice student may "hate cops" due to anger about police violence and believe police are corrupt and untrustworthy. They may "hate criminals." The physics student does not feel this way about her subject matter. While a criminal justice student may hate cops the physics student has no such sentiment; she does not hate atoms or momentum (although she may dislike learning about them). The angry student who hates cops will be unlikely to impartially process information about policing. The student who hates "criminals" is unlikely to be receptive to ideas related to rehabilitation or prisoner reentry. For effective criminal justice education, students need to be aware of the emotions aroused by criminal justice issues and how these influence their thinking. The emotional nature of criminal justice is important and is typically overlooked in criminal justice education.

The effect of ideology is also important and neglected in introductory texts. The subject matter of criminal justice makes its study particularly vulnerable to ideological influence that hinders effective learning. Our definition of ideology is shaped by a number of factors, but evidence concerning "confirmation bias" is illustrative. That is, there is a good deal of evidence that once formed, beliefs are highly resistant to information or evidence challenging them and belief holders are likely to ignore contradictory evidence or interpret it in a way that maintains their existing belief system (Nickerson, 1998). *This is what we mean by ideology—a set of beliefs that once established in a person's mind interferes with the way she or he deals with information, especially information challenging her or his beliefs.* Clearly there are many types of ideology (religious, political), and these will have a varying impact upon how a person processes information. The more strongly an ideology is held the greater its impact upon information processing and so the person with an immutable ideology interprets information in a manner consistent with that ideology, whereas a person with a malleable ideology may be more likely to reevaluate their worldviews in the face of new information. There is good reason to believe criminal justice majors are especially likely to enter their field of study with strong ideological beliefs that may impact their ability to objectively evaluate information (e.g., Johnson, 2009; Moons & Mackie, 2007; Hurley & Hurley, 2015; Karstedt, 2002; Wimshurst et al., 2004). We have no concern over what our students' ideological beliefs are, only with the effect of ideology upon their ability to impartially examine and evaluate information. We believe it is essential for criminal justice students to become aware of their ideological beliefs—not to change them, but to understand how their beliefs influence their thinking and how ideology makes them resistant to information that questions it. We believe that this awareness will better prepare students for more objective analysis of criminal justice policies and practices. To that end, throughout the text we hope to raise awareness of the impact of ideology and pay particularly close attention to it in Chapter 4.

This text does not provide an exhaustive examination of criminal justice topics. Instead we focus on what we believe are issues fundamental to the study of crime and justice. By focusing on the issues examined here it is our hope readers will expand their critical thinking abilities and apply them when examining other criminal justice topics. It is our firm belief that criminal justice is a dynamic discipline that must constantly be examined, evaluated, and changed if we are to produce a system that can promote justice and make communities safer for us all.

CHAPTER 2

JUSTICE AND SACRIFICE

This is a chapter on justice, sacrifice, and liberty. First: justice. We do not assume that we all share the same definition of justice—we do not assume that our system is in fact just. In truth, we all should assume very little. Even if you believe that individuals act with the best of intentions, you should still be cautious in assuming they act without error. Our justice system can always be improved. But who are we as a people—who are we as a society? What do we want—as individuals and as a collective? What do we find meaningful and important, what do we value? To begin this discussion, we turn to justice and begin to articulate a clearer understanding of the proposition.

We use the term "justice" in serious conversation. You have probably heard people demand it on the streets; you may have heard remarks expressing its requirement in court rooms, on television, on the radio. We do believe that there is a general sense that we are all talking about a similar thing—but are we talking about the same thing? We seem to pay little attention to precisely what we are talking about—is justice simply restitution or retribution? Is our personal understanding of justice what the collective requires? How do the demands of individual actors mesh with the demands of the state? Can our understanding of justice be appropriately sophisticated and nuanced so that it defends individuals, neighborhoods, cities, and the nation as a whole? Have we sacrificed a faint idea—a notion—for a concrete and useful tool? We find it unfortunate that Criminal Justice texts do not provide adequate discussion of justice and what we require from the laws we create. We admit that justice is a challenging proposition. And it is possible that our discussion will generate many more questions. But living with a certain degree of uncertainty keeps the mind awake and inquisitive. Once objects (and propositions) are defined we tend to store them and do not allow them to be easily redefined. We should always pursue the discussion of justice—and do so rigorously. But keep in mind that this is not an exhaustive discussion of justice. That would be a near impossible task. Instead, this is a guide that suggests one way to gain further understanding of what we want when we demand justice.

As you all enter the field, you will be repeatedly faced with decisions that can dramatically impact the lives of individuals. There is great responsibility in work that pursues and defends justice. It is a great commitment and sacrifice—and it asks for a *serious inquiry into the nature and complexity of justice*. Knowing what to ask is key to solving problems. The answer may never be the same but the approach to obtain the answer will be.

To begin this discussion, let's turn to Sigmund Freud.

Freud (1930) suggests that justice is that no one is above the law: "A law once made will not be broken in favour of an individual" (1930, p. 49). This is a useful place to begin because it seems to be sufficient. We are all equal before the law. We could spend some time and observe the practices of our society and very quickly we could conclude—perhaps even without strict analysis (though we rarely condone this)—whether or not we believe our society to be just or unjust. Are certain types of people less likely to be punished by the justice system? Do certain groups seem to receive preferential treatment? If certain groups do receive preferential treatment, if select individuals do appear to evade the consequences of law breaking, then we may have a problem. Some members *appear* to be above the law.

So we begin with one central question:

> Do we *believe/perceive/imagine* that certain definable groups are above the law?

Most of us start with celebrities or other people with means. We have read stories about famous men and women evading prison, receiving suspended sentences, acquittals in the face of overwhelming evidence. We might even consider specific cases; for example, suppose we consider the Stanford student who was convicted of rape and then granted a 6-month prison sentence. Our first reaction may be anger, frustration, incredulity. Our next reaction may be a quick comparison. We may compare the Stanford case to the Vanderbilt football team case (multiple members of the football team were convicted of rape and sentenced to lengthy prison terms). But we do not need to follow this exact path—we could consider Lindsay Lohan and compare her treatment to that of a classmate, or a friend, or even ourselves. We may consider a variety of newsworthy events and connect the dots to personal experience or to other events in different towns or states. But the process is similar. We are forming an opinion of the treatment of people in our society. These observations, however, do not indicate that certain groups are in fact above the law. This is our *perception*—and this perception might be based on unintentionally biased media coverage or oversaturation of certain stories. This perception might be based on personal experience that is not representative of overall treatment or experiences. Certainly, our own experiences may be distinct and unique in this fashion—but they also might not be. What sorts of stories and examples do we privilege (this very question is discussed in detail in our Chapter 4 on media)? In addition, we might overlook countless examples of leniency that are not considered newsworthy because the actors are not known entities.

Here, it is important to note that even if we are incorrect, the *perception* that certain groups are above the law—or receive preferential treatment—can serve to undermine the system itself.

We will return to this idea multiple times, from a variety of angles. But for now, keep in mind that this is a question about fairness—or legitimacy. And this leads us to another critical question:

> Do you believe the criminal justice system is legitimate and can this impact the actual administration of justice?

Legitimacy is a profoundly important proposition that asks whether or not the system itself treats people fairly *and* whether or not those people perceive their treatment to be fair. But why should we care if people *perceive* treatment to be fair? After all, these are empirical questions that can be addressed by science. We can ask and find out whether or not people are processed differently depending on race, gender, age, and so on. If the results of countless studies indicate that there is no difference in arrest and incarceration practices based on identity characteristics then this should justify justice practices. But, reasonably or not, this is not adequate. Justice is not merely reflective of an objective reality. There is a subjective component. Subjective does not suggest irrational or impossible to quantify. Instead, it suggests that the perceived experiences of people are important for justice actors to consider while conducting their work. One issue is that if certain types of people do not perceive their treatment to be fair, then they are less likely to perceive the system to be legitimate and this diminishes belief in the law. This is a tough pill for many people to swallow. Until we consider the political landscape in the United States. Populations continually feel that their rights are threatened—right to own guns, right to marriage, right to an abortion, right to privacy. The list is endless and occupies all corners of the political spectrum. If policies in the legislature seem to favor one group over another then the perception of the system itself can be harmed because a change in policy does not change anyone's opinion on whatever right is being denied or expanded. But it could change the alienated group's opinion of the legislature itself. The danger with perception is that it can undermine institutions themselves and this can undermine the ability for these institutions to complete necessary work. If you do not trust the police are you going to cooperate with the police? If our perception is tainted, we do not need to actively break the law to harm the system. We can withhold our cooperation, remove ourselves from public forums, change our routines and practices. Belief in the justice system is essential because the justice system requires the public to solve crimes, to improve punishment and reentry practices, and establish meaningful victim support strategies.

How the system operates and how the public—across all populations—*perceives* the system to operate does actually matter. You might be thinking at this point: *Justice actors have an impossible job. There is no way that we can be concerned with our actual work* ***and*** *the perception of our actual work*. But we must be. And both of these are empirical questions that can be understood through data analysis and remedied through changes in practice. We can understand our impact and the perception of our impact through research. If we listen to this research (and demand that it is conducted), we can improve our practices and the meaning in our own work. But furthering our own understanding of justice—and punishment—first requires us to commit to the inquiry and second requires us to communicate our findings to the world (especially when we are justice actors). It is not sufficient for a particular innovation or program to work. The approach must be based on an overall narrative that reflects who we are as a society.

Let's return to Freud.

We could argue that Freud's definition is more expansive than "no one is above the law."

Inherent in Freud's definition is the idea that an unjust law would be a law that favors certain individuals and an unjust state would be one that favors certain people—be they rich, White, male, Christian. You might think that this inference is unreasonable. But if a law cannot be broken in favor of an individual how can a law be made in favor of an individual? Allowing this form of law construction would privilege certain people and would essentially nullify the power of Freud's definition. Select individuals—or groups—could simply write laws that favor their own self-interest. Of course, this does happen but the fact that this happens only demonstrates that the civilization or the society is not as just as it needs to be—it has not, in short, met the "first requisite of civilization" (Freud, 1930, p. 49). As Freud well knows, civilization is a work in progress. We are moving toward a more perfected state.

For the state to be just, thereby, laws cannot be written to favor people for who they are; just laws are written to define what people can and cannot do. There is an action required. Just practices must be based on actions and we also must act to be unjust. But in that action, we have not yet reached a reasonable conclusion as to what justice is. Is Freud suggesting that since no one is above the law the law must be equally enforced across all populations—that, in a sense, the law must be formally rational: Crime x receives punishment y? Or does an individual—and by extension, a certain group—have a right to introduce context into the situation. Does an individual (and again a group) have the right to introduce situational factors—both within the course of committing a particular act (*I was starving; it was self-defense*) and within the general conditions of societal inequality (*we have no resources; we have terrible schools*)? Could justice ever be a reflection of contextual realities or societal inequalities?

We could argue that everyone is the same before the law. But if there is no need for me to break the law to feed my family—and there is a need for another to break the law to feed her family—doesn't this law, by definition, violate Freud's definition (at least in our extension)? The situational factors, thereby, have created a situation in which the law works the same for all involved but does not respect the starting position of all those involved. Would this be a just society? If not, then how would I fairly write a law that took into account resource distribution, perhaps even racial and gender discrimination, and did not then excuse certain people for their actions because of who they are? Are people less culpable because of who they are? This again appears to fly in the face of Freud's demand. We also appear to be at an impasse. We probably do not want to openly admit that you are less responsible for breaking the law because of available resources but we also understand that certain situations probably do deserve leniency. There are, indeed, aggravating circumstances. So what do we do?

It appears that we want discretion to play some role here. We want the officer, the judge, to hear our side of the story. We want our context and those vital mitigating factors to actually work in our favor. When we are in trouble we seem to demand that we are heard—and go so far as to claim that the system is unjust if it does not listen to us (and in most instances agree with us). So is justice an individual perception that the state must always take our side and must always side with our "group"? We are not sure anyone would agree with that definition. How do we acknowledge individual circumstance and allow for uniform enforcement and protection?

The issue might be that we don't understand why we have agreed to live in the collective social state. Why do we give up so much to be part of society?

SACRIFICE

We make sacrifices when we agree to live within the confines of society. We are asked to play by rules, to adhere to norms, and violating many of these norms and rules is punishable by law. The law can often seem arbitrary, even unfair. There are countless examples of men and women who have appeared to circumvent the law; there are countless examples of men and women who are disproportionately targeted by justice practices.

There are far too many reasons to dislike the system itself: violations of rights; government overreach; infringement of liberties; unreasonable resource allocation.

Is the sacrifice worth it? Do we actually get more out of this agreement than we give to it? Social membership does come with cost. But the cost of membership is preferable to the world dictated without societal safeguards. This does not suggest that all costs are worth membership nor does it suggest that certain costs are unreasonable (or even unfair and/or violate our individual liberty). But this does indicate that "society" is preferable to "not-society." Indeed, our real problems are only solved *through* the collective (Freud, 1930). We can make it better; we can extract greater liberty. We probably do not want to run from it.

The social contract is a difficult proposition. We do not actually sign a contract with society. The social contract is not a formal document (although perhaps it should be). *The social contract, therefore, does not exist.* But it does represent a powerful illustration as to why we want to bridge the gap from absolute freedom to restricted freedom. Consider the construction of the social contract and agreement to its terms like any thought experiment. The purpose is to begin to understand what questions we need to ask and how to philosophically approach problems with productive results that protect us each equally (and preserve our individual liberty). The foundation of society justifies punishment. Therefore, we need to construct a reasonable argument for society in order to begin to defend a rationale of punishment. This process will also allow us to select an appropriate punishment philosophy and an appropriate punishment practice.

Remember: there is no morality in nature.

Morality is a choice and it is a choice that we must continually make. The laws we make tell us who we are and what behaviors we consider to be "right" and what behaviors we consider to be "wrong." We do not outlaw that which is impossible; we outlaw choices that we believe people should not make. We tell one another that murder is "wrong" (although we excuse it in many contexts); we do not tell people that turning people into ants is wrong. However, if this becomes possible we might decide to outlaw the behavior—but only when it becomes a *possible* choice. This is important because as the world changes, as technology changes, as our abilities change, our morality also changes. It may not be a fundamental shift in who we are and what we value but rather a recategorization as to how we protect what we value (but it also could be a fundamental shift in who we are and what we value).

As we move through definitions of "good" and "bad" behavior this will become clear. But for now, let us address the foundation itself and answer the simple question: *why form society?* As thought experiments go, let us begin with a simple story:

> An elderly man, let us call him George, takes a walk in the woods with a backpack filled with gold coins. *The largest and strongest man in the world* sees George in the woods and tells George to give him the backpack. George refuses. *The largest and strongest man in the world* punches George in the face and walks away with the bag. Later, *the largest and strongest man in the world* falls asleep next to a river and a young child appears and quietly takes the backpack with the gold coins and runs into the woods.

The inhabitants of this world are unhappy. In part, they are unhappy because events like the above event continue to occur without repercussion. They are also unhappy because strength does not give them protection or "rights"—and they are unhappy because they have no recourse, no way to protect themselves and their loved ones. They are limited by who they are. As humans they age, they can get sick, and they die. They must eat and they must sleep. The body itself limits what we are capable of doing. But the natural world also inflicts pain on the living—earthquakes, hurricanes, tornadoes, winter. Keep in mind that nature did not prevent any of the above acts from occurring. There is nothing in nature that precludes murder—indeed, it is essential to the animal kingdom's survival. There is nothing in nature that restricts theft, rape, arson, burglary. These are *social* restrictions. These are restrictions on what choices we are "allowed" to make and what choices we are not "allowed" to make. It is possible for one person to kill another person. Nature does not prevent it.

Therefore, this simple story asks us to consider a series of questions about punishment (and our society in general):

a. How should we define "right" and "wrong"?
b. What rules are we agreeing to when we join and live in a civilized society?
c. How should we apprehend and punish offenders?

And if we consider this story in further detail we are forced to consider even more interesting questions:

1. What responsibility does society have to (a) punish and (b) honor the punishment?
2. What does the public demand from punishment and will the public accept reason (empirical realities over "gut" realities).

People do not like it when others can steal their material possessions or harm their physical skin with impunity. But, technically, a world with absolute freedom would not restrict this type of behavior. Morality is consumed by choice. Natural law already restricts the human animal and then allows it to act, as it desires within those confines. In the world described above, all the actors have complete freedom. Indeed, they have *absolute* freedom to do as they please. Their actions are not controlled by external forces. The only factors that control their abilities are natural factors. The old man is old—and maybe age has brought unfortunate realities with it: diminished eyesight, weaker muscles, slow reaction time. The largest man is strong and powerful and intimidating. At least, when he is awake. But he cannot stay awake forever. He still needs to sleep (and eat) and therefore he can still be prey to a less large individual—even to a child. This immense man can still become sick, he can still break, he is still vulnerable to the natural world and therefore, within the correct set of fortunate—or unfortunate—circumstances he can become a victim of a "crime." This is an important clarification because even the most selfish and greedy of persons would still prefer to have some sort of societal protection so that she may pursue her desire of amassing excessive material gain. This proposition holds even for the worst of us—even for our worst qualities—we still want to cede freedom to the state, in return for protection.

The above story is somewhat tame. Imagine, instead, a less contrived existence with the above rules. An existence where murder and rape and assault are frequent; where the physically stronger prey on the physically weaker—and where even the physically stronger are subject to sleep, food shortages, sickness, and, *if lucky*, aging. Our physical realities and limitations actually generate a world where life by ourselves, life where we only respond to our own passions and to our own desires is actually a miserable life. It is an unhappy existence. But because we can reason because we are human we can find a way out of this unhappy state. Our way out, however, requires equal protection in order to provide individual protection. And this holds even for the worst of us—the vilest, greediest, most savage, and monstrous of neighbors. Because even he wants to be part of this collective; even he will sacrifice to join this collective. The gains are so substantial, the rewards tangible, the protections real.

But we do not want to give up our freedom to another *person* because we know that we have the potential to be monstrous (and the potential to be greedy and selfish). If we give up our freedom to another person, in exchange for security and protection, then we are held to the mercy of another individual who may be even worse than we are. There is nothing requiring this person to be serious and pragmatic. Her desires could be whimsical, her nature capricious, and her demands irrational, contradictory, and unreasonable. Instead of ceding freedom to a realized idea we have ceded freedom to a person and trusted that person to protect our self-interest. But there is no obligation for that person to honor that trust or to protect the rights of individual members of the state.

We cannot blindly trust strength if we care about our individual rights.

More to the point, strength is independent of morality. A strong person may be moral but she or he is not required to be moral. Strength does not represent any specific set of ethics. Strength is merely force; if I am strong I can bend you to my will but my will is not required to bend to any sort of ideology (good or bad). Therefore, if I am the strongest person I may demand that all *men* cannot leave their homes. And if I am strong enough I could enforce this demand. However, when I am replaced by the next strongest person (after I die or am bested), she or he may demand that all *women* cannot leave their homes. She or he too would be able to enforce the new demand. Both decrees would be enforced by strength. But the decrees are in direct opposition to one another. There is nothing but the will itself that is required to enforce it and my will is not required to adhere to anything but itself. This is the general meaning of "might does not make right." As the basis of a state in which each member would want to be a part—a powerful proposition—this is not sufficient. I would not want to join a club that could not tell me its rules or its reason for existence. I would not want to join a club that would change its very nature, rationale, and purpose every time its leadership changed.

But there are clubs I would want to join. When the power is transferred away from the *individual*—away from "man" or "king"—and toward the *collective* then the strength lies among the communion of persons. Instead of rule of man we have rule of law, and the rule of law, as considered in this thought experiment, protects each person equally. If effective and meaningful, law has allegiance only to itself. It owes its existence to the state but cannot be useful unless it bows only to itself. Regardless of who we are, we are protected by the law equally and the law does not—and cannot—have a capricious will. (Remember: this is a thought experiment and allows us to understand how the law *should* operate.) If the law did not provide as much protection for us as it did our neighbors, we would not agree to the state that gave birth to the law. The contract itself only works, and can only operate, if we all agree to its premise of equal sacrifice. Through collective consensus, of which we are all an equal part and have equal protection, the agreement (by definition) is legitimate.

Keep in mind that our own thought experiment borrows heavily from social theorists such as Jean-Jacques Rousseau and criminologists such as Cesare Beccaria but is not necessarily a mirror image. No one "owns" the social contract. We make arguments as to why it is preferable to obey the general will that is directly reflective of our own will and we stand on the shoulders of those who have made particularly strong arguments in the past. But society itself, in order to fulfill this dream, must be continually ours. The social contract must be ours—understood, endorsed, and advanced by us. Even if the contract is just a symbol. If we remember the symbol then we remember our necessary role in civic participation. The symbol, in this way, becomes active.

Of course, all this does not preclude the possibility that certain individuals will reject the membership. So, what if I don't want to join?

We could infer that membership should be voluntary since involuntary servitude and fealty brings to mind unfortunate comparisons to slavery (and we make the assumption that no rational person would willingly accept enslavement). Indeed, willful participation is not an unfortunate condition. If membership is voluntary and offered to each person who is willing to sacrifice natural freedom then those who form the collective are, without suspicion, equal partners. And those who do not join do not reap the benefits of the collective. This includes not only physical protection but also protection of property, protection of *rights*—civil liberties. Our sacrifice gives us civil liberties. Our sacrifice is what makes the state and the government exist. Without our sacrifice there is no state and there is no government. If we cease to sacrifice natural freedom then the state is dissolved. It cannot exist without this sacrifice. Therefore, we cannot permit members to gain the benefits of the state without also sharing in the sacrifice. This would undermine the entire proposition. So, we must address this problem directly. We must, in some form, sanction those who resist our compact. We must force those who refuse to accept our conditions to accept our conditions. And we achieve this through punishment (which we discuss in detail in Chapter 3).

It would seem reasonable that those who refuse to accept our conditions and no longer wish to be protected by our collective can be exiled (perhaps even executed—but that is another conversation). There could, in this scenario, be a mutual break. We no longer wish to be bed fellows. Presumably, the person who rejects our offer also accepts the consequence: she or he will not be granted our protection and our benefits.

So what if I violate the social contract *as a member of the state*?

The premise of this question acknowledges at least two possibilities: people who have violated the public trust and still wish to be protected by the state and people who have violated the public trust and no longer wish to be protected. It is necessary to recognize these two populations but it is not necessary to handle their violation differently. Since both were members of the state at the time of the violation it becomes the obligation of the state to address the infractions similarly (otherwise I could opt out of membership if I were to get "caught"; therefore, the incentive to break the rules would be part of the arrangement and the contract would no longer be tenable). So, let us treat each population the same.

Those who have violated our contract have failed to maintain their sacrifice. They have failed to adhere to our "new" adopted morality. It may be appropriate for some of these individuals to be reassimilated, but it is imperative for all of them to be punished in such a manner that those who have not violated the public trust and have made great investment in the formation and maintenance of the state are adequately "compensated."

This line of reasoning is similar to the following: I should be rewarded for playing by the rules. And I should see that you are punished for breaking the rules. Otherwise, there is little incentive for me to play by the rules.

This raises another dilemma: how should we punish the offender?

At this point, assume that our state is healthy and productive. It is prospering and the members believe in it. Moreover, the members *run* it. The sacrifice that forms the state is equally felt across all persons and all persons take ownership seriously. Let us also assume that the government that oversees this prosperous state is in fact made up of each sacrificing member. The government has not replaced the individual—it is the collection of all individuals. We admit that this becomes difficult to imagine when the population of the state—or country—becomes large. But in many ways the larger the population the more necessary this condition becomes. It is precisely the anonymity and the distance from governing that begins to generate isolation and powerlessness—a disconnect from the gears of power and a feeling that one is unable to shape outcomes. Our thought experiment is designed to resist just such an outcome. In this scenario, the power never leaves the individual because the state exists due to her sacrifice and the sacrifice of all her neighbors. *It only exists because of the sacrifice.* Without the sacrifice there is no government and there is no state. And each of them has sacrificed equally. No one, thereby, is by law superior.

So how do we punish?

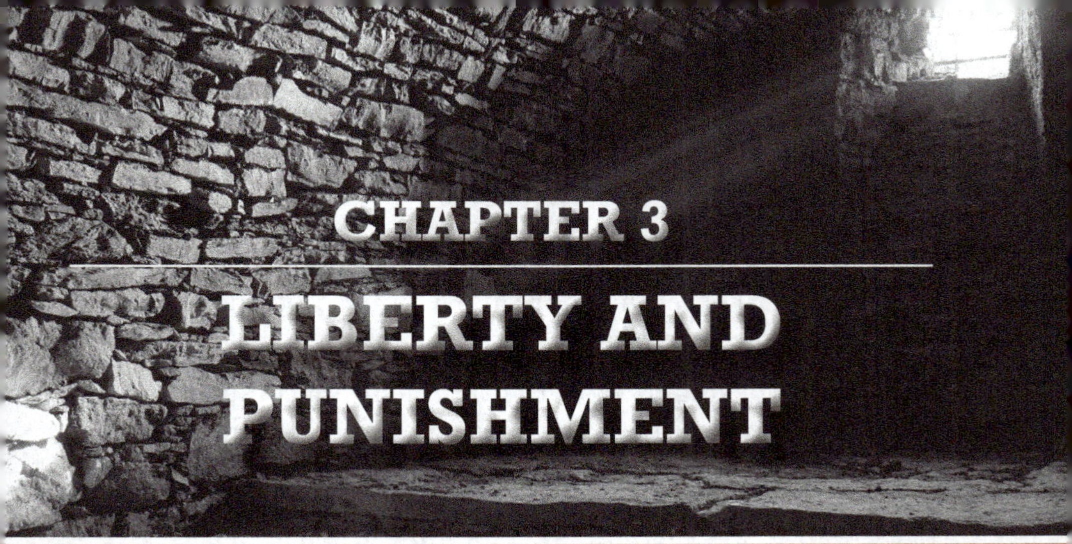

CHAPTER 3

LIBERTY AND PUNISHMENT

So how should we punish?

How should we punish those who decided to violate the social contract? We have to acknowledge that our club—in this case the state itself—has bestowed considerable benefits to those of us who have played by the rules. Not only are we given protection by the government but we are also given protection *from* the government.

It may be helpful to remember that in our own thought experiment we are the government. The state does not exist, in this scenario, unless we create it and we create it by establishing certain "rules." Since the government only exists because we have willed it and these "rules" are by definition the government, it follows that if the government were to violate these rules it would be, in essence, dissolving itself. This thought experiment is useful in terms of understanding why we want government (or less freedom) and how we ensure that our rights—that which we hold sacred—are protected.

To sum up:

> If:
>
> > Government = Our sacrifice of natural freedoms in exchange for civil liberties + property

Then:

> If we no longer have civil liberties then we no longer have an ideal government because we want protection by and *from* the government.

Obviously, the quality of our government is a complex and potentially confusing situation. Absent civil liberties, we would still have some form of government in the *real world.* But this government would no longer be representing our best interest and therefore it would not be ideal. We want protection by the government. But we also want protection *from* the government (consider privacy as an example). Yet only a regulated system can provide each of these outcomes. Government per se is not the issue but the type of government may be. It is important to distinguish between those who are arguing for more or fewer regulations and those who are arguing for "government" or "no government." The "no government" factions reflect anarchy: it should be clear we do not reject government, our concern is with its function. Debating the size of government is better understood as reasonable differences of opinion between rational political entities. For example, one party might want to spend more on national defense and less on social welfare, while another party might want to do the exact opposite. This is a debate about type and size of government rather than the existence or demise of government itself.

The entire political establishment exists within government. This point is often lost. *Outrage at practices by the government—generally because those practices do not reflect the interests or values of a particular group—are different than outrages at government itself.* Often, these two are conflated. It is vital that we do not make this mistake although it is common to do so. For example, publicized atrocities by police might make some "hate the police" but this position confuses distaste for police actions with the institution itself—wanting no police violence is not an argument for no police.

Regardless of our particular individual values—and there is considerable variation among Americans on values—the state itself is essential to the individual's happiness. The exercise here attempts to illustrate a useful thought experiment through which we can critique the current system in terms of its perfection (and in terms of its possibility). If simple protections are not afforded to all, and to all in similar fashion and extent, then the current status of the state is imperfect. Not necessarily unfixable but certainly not ideal. By design, the law should protect each citizen exactly the same and no one should be above or beyond the reach of the law. Due to contextual factors, our blameworthiness and therefore our punishments might vary, but our treatment or *processing* should not.

To clarify, through the social contract, we gain protection of property and protection of ourselves *by* the government; but the social contract also gives us civil liberties—or protection *from* the government. We conceded absolute freedom in order to gain these protections and rights. Remember: we did not hand over our freedom to some entity—individual or body. Each of us willingly gives up our natural freedom in exchange for civil liberties and property. And because we each have the same at stake—we have sacrificed the same thing in size and scope—each of us should receive the same return. Here is the heart of the social contract, we give up unlimited freedom and gain liberty. Liberty is adhering to the rules we ourselves write, rules that protect all of us equally and to which we all have an interest in maintaining (see Rousseau, 1762).

So where does punishment fit in all of this?

The rules only work if they are enforced. By agreeing to the social contract (generally implicitly), we have preserved—or perhaps protected the birth and survival of—our self-interest. Our ability to arbitrarily and violently interfere in our neighbors' lives has been eagerly and willingly abandoned (read: outlawed). Our new pact therefore allows us to live in relative peace, to raise a family, to pursue professional careers that are only possible within civilization. Our collective society, now complete with countless pathways toward individual meaning and satisfaction, allows for the development of science, the treatment and cure of disease, the division of labor, the diversification of opportunities and occupations, the protection from nature's wrath. Our pact has likewise ensured numerous pathways to happiness (and, of course, misery). But generally, we citizens acknowledge, maybe only casually or even subconsciously, that the fix to all our problems and future problems is only possible through the collective—our happiness is only possible within the collective. We cannot build careers, lose ourselves in art, make money, pursue self-interest beyond the base appetites of our animal ancestors without the social state. Laws make it possible to hold transgressors accountable and protect commerce, industry, and human identity. Laws allow for the entire infrastructure of the state to maintain itself inviolate.

But, again, the laws must be enforced.

Even though it is in our best interest to obey the laws we have prescribed to ourselves—laws that protect us from our neighbors and ensure we are treated equally and fairly—there is often occasion where breaking the law helps us to reach our goals more quickly. Because the regulated state has potentially created a great wealth of opportunity, it is easy to see how a goal of economic success could quickly overwhelm the *appropriate or legal* means to obtain such success. Since the state now offers a series of lucrative opportunities, and money can purchase items that suit our desires, it is possible that our desire for monetary success may outmaneuver our own desire to play by the rules—*even though those rules are the only reason the state exists in the first place*. We are selfish and greedy individuals (some of us, many of us). When we lose sight of the value of the foundation of our society then it is easier for us to seek to manipulate the rules to suit our self-interest. It is possible that this is inevitable. It is possible that this is human nature. But human nature also seeks self-preservation above all else. Indeed, without the self, there is nothing. Logically, it is difficult to argue for an item of greater value than the self (particularly to the self-interested individual). For many of us, the divide between our own self-interest and the collective interest invested in the state itself—not in a particular form of government but in government itself—is substantial. But if we can remember that the state is the sum of our sacrifice and we are the government then we may be able to understand that flaws in legal codes or in access to protection are flaws within the current framework of the state and not within the idea of government itself. To help us remember, playing by the rules must be encouraged, esteemed, and championed. We need to hold those accountable who violate the contract—our mutual sacrifice—and remind the offenders why adherence to our agreement is necessary and in *their* best interest. We also must punish the offenders so that those who are playing by the rules, who are pursuing legal avenues to obtain the benefits available through our collective, believe that their investment and sacrifice is worth it. If we are sacrificing freedom to this "club," then we must believe that the sacrifice is worthwhile and that the benefits of membership outweigh the costs of the sacrifice.

But if the sacrifice is not equally felt or not equally required across populations then this entire foundation is challenged. What we sacrifice—what we give up—must be equal to what you sacrificed and to what each protected member has sacrificed.

In essence, we have joined a club that allows us to maintain our individual identity as long as we incorporate the simple and agreeable social mandate: do not harm your neighbor. Eventually, a regulatory body may be necessary to determine the intent, extent, and existence of harm; but at its most base level the simple condition of "do no harm" illustrates the powerful reality that *we have really conceded nothing that we want and in return have gained everything that we do want*. The freedom that we sacrifice in the social contract is not the freedom that we want. The freedom we want is *liberty*—the freedom to pursue our own paths, discover who we actually are, live our lives unfettered by *arbitrary* government interference.

And arbitrary is key here: when we enter into the social contract we accept a level of government interference—it may not be desirable although it is necessary—but the rules must apply and be enforced equally. We do not perceive a just or legitimate government to be one that, for the same actions, intrudes in our lives but not yours, punishes us but not you. But this does not suggest that for each illicit act the actor receives the *same* punishment. Context is inherent in punishment; context is part of the evaluation of the severity of behavior. The crux of this position is that—like justice—punishment is dialogic. Meting out fair punishments requires balancing the needs of the victim, the blameworthiness of the offender, and the needs of the state. In and of itself, this should not trouble us. People are different: children are *different* than adults; a woman who is blind is *different* than a woman with sight; an individual with substantial cognitive impairment is *different* than an individual with normal cognitive functioning. Hence, this also means that motivation for illicit acts varies among individuals and as motivation varies so does blameworthiness. Ultimately, the solution is to find a way to treat *like cases alike* and to transparently convey that treatment to the public. Consistency in how we react to *like* cases is key here and fairness requires us to consider the totality of circumstances in evaluating action.

Presumably, we do not want the freedom to murder with impunity because that freedom allows our neighbors the equivalent freedom to murder us and so we live in fear, with uncertainty. But it is possible that certain actors do want such a freedom. What we do to these actors is critical. Those who want the freedom that we willfully cede (the freedom to murder, rob, etc.) are easily vilified as monsters, *traitors*. These are the men and women who want to do harm to us and to members of our society. And these men and women *must* be punished because if they are not then the social contract will crumble. They have attacked the very fabric of our happiness; they have attacked all that allows us to be happy. It is reasonable for us to hate them and to wish for great harm to come to them. Indeed, if we do not punish them then our sacrifice means nothing and our compact means nothing because it is not and apparently cannot be enforced.

But we must be careful.

Punishment must increase solidarity *not reduce* solidarity. Punishment must not generate an "us" versus "them" reality. If we are not measured in our punishment practices we run the risk of generating a condition that terrifies the average citizen. Physical harm—or torture—of neighbors does little but display the awesome power of the state. That display divides us and diminishes the power, the influence, of the social contract. It is probably advisable to flesh out this point. If someone disrespected all that you value and did it in such a way that caused all you value to disappear how would you feel? How would you want to react?

> *Or in more direct terms:*
>
> Barbara Burglar breaks into your house and steals your television and your bed and your stove.
>
> > Question: how harshly would you want the state to respond to these crimes? What would you want to happen to Ms. Burglar?
>
> *Or more viciously:*
>
> Murdon Murderer murders your friend and it makes the news because it is gruesome.
>
> > Question: How would you want the state to respond to this crime? What would you want to happen to Mr. Murderer?

Take a few seconds and mentally note your responses to the above hypotheticals. Now consider a different set of scenarios at your current college or university.

1. Chester Cheater cheats on an exam and gets caught.

   Question: How should the university approach this action—what would be reasonable and what would be an unreasonable response?

Or perhaps more egregious:

2. Matt Acid gets caught with heroin possession
3. Jessica A. Salt gets caught physically assaulting her roommate

If we begin with the campus examples a series of responses may have occurred to you and these responses were probably reasonable given the situation. You may have even insisted on gaining further information about the conditions and the context under which these events took place. This is a logical and fair demand—a dialogue between the student, the student body, and the university is essential. The process of dialogic engagement demonstrates a dedication to fairness—fairness requires that we consider context in evaluating behavior so *outcomes for different actors engaging in similar behaviors can differ, they may do so often, once we consider the totality of the circumstances surrounding the behavior. The key is that outcomes not differ arbitrarily.* But this is not our purpose at present. Here, the main objective is to understand what type of punishment would *alienate* members of the community. Regardless of guilt, is it possible that the university itself could undermine its authority by handling these cases (a) too leniently or (b) too strictly? Suppose that there was no punishment for any of the above acts that presumably violate the honor code at most universities in the United States. If the cheater is caught and there is no consequence, what does that say about cheating? What does that say about breaking the rules? What does that say about the university, the collective? A reasonable person would argue that an illicit action without consequences would indicate that the rules are not important and therefore the work and the sacrifice required to play by the rules have been greatly diminished.

Or:

No consequence to unwanted action = No incentive to act within the rules.

But this is not the entire story. As the crime changes does the appropriate action become murkier?

Broadly speaking, many of you may insist that cheating and using drugs are very different types of rule violation. Matt's own drug use could even be considered his own problem. However, Chester's cheating attacks the very integrity of the academic institution and, ultimately, the diplomas it confers each year. Students work toward a transferrable piece of paper that is only as strong as the university and is arguably therefore only as strong as the integrity of the university and its practices.

But academic interests are not the same as personal interests. Like crimes, all university violations are not equal.

If drug possession does violate the student code of conduct, then it is probably reasonable for some action to be taken against Matt for possession. But does drug possession harm the university's integrity in the *same way* as cheating? Does drug possession cause harm to the collective? What type of response is reasonable and what type of response goes too far? Do you think the person you sit next to in class would agree with your perspective? What about the person sitting across from you? Note: as in Chapter 1, we are again asking you to question your assumptions, how you typically think about rule violation. Through education, through media, we are told of the dangers of drugs (and these are real), and so we punish drug violations heavily. That is, our experience leads us to think in terms of specific acts and how they *should* be punished (e.g., drug use should be severely punished, assault should be severely punished, cheating on an exam not so much). Our experience does not lead us to think about the greater purpose or effects of punishment.

People acting in good faith probably will not agree with (a) the level of harm caused by each action *or* (b) the suitable reaction to each action. And yet the university—and in similar fashion the law—must react to violations of its code of conduct. Depending on the reaction, the status of the university may be greatly improved or greatly diminished. Unfortunately, the student body may view administrators' actions very differently than alumni or the general public.

The import of this discussion is (a) the value and necessity of punishment and (b) the necessity to consider potential reactions to the punishment.

The first point relates to maintaining social order—a vital component of punishment. The second point relates to maintaining legitimacy, or perceived fair and equal treatment across populations. This is primarily a chapter directed at the first point. But legitimacy deficiencies may undermine the actions of sanctioning agents, so it is important to include perception of treatment in this discussion.

One way to rationally resolve this issue is to classify violations in terms of harm. The legal system classifies felonies on a lettered scale, generally ending at A, as the most serious. But what should be the *basis* for that scale? The scale is important because it introduces consistency and, presumably, allows for the creation of reasonable punishment guidelines. We do not want to punish arbitrarily; we do not want to let emotion or prejudice influence punishment. Eventually arbitrary punishment makes us question the legitimacy of the punishing body. But we do not simply want to adopt measures because they seem to be sufficient and well organized. We need to understand the rationale for such an adoption. *What is the general argument that supports such a scale.*

Let us assume that we would like to classify violations in terms of harm. To streamline this conversation, let us also assume that there are two main sources of harm that students can inflict upon a university (ignoring, perhaps irresponsibly but only for this truncated discussion, property damage):

A. Harm to the safety of students, faculty, and staff

B. Harm to the university's academic integrity

We begin with what we consider to be the most harmful act against the university's academic integrity: cheating. Cheating challenges the integrity of the university *if it is not sanctioned.* The university has a vested interest in eliminating—or at least dramatically reducing—incidents of cheating. A university that does not demonstrate significant effort toward eliminating student cheating is not legitimate as no one can be sure a graduate of that institution learned their subject matter or, perhaps more importantly, is willing to make the necessary sacrifice to play by the rules (study, write, meet deadlines).

But keep in mind, the university would not be able to refer this matter to the criminal justice system. Chester would not be facing criminal charges for cheating on an exam (the state could adopt criminal statutes against college cheating, but this is unlikely since general consensus would probably see this as merely bad taste—deviant instead of criminal behavior). Chester will not end up in prison for cheating on an exam.

So how should the university proceed? What would be the best way for the university to maintain its integrity *and* maintain its appeal to potential and current students (as well as to the general public and to alumni)? How could all these parties be placated?

Consider the example of student Salt, caught assaulting her roommate. Suppose the university decided to act against the student in the same way that the student acted against a member of the university. Suppose the university decided that student Salt deserved to be formally assaulted by the dean as a form of retribution, or eye-for-an-eye. After all, retribution is often appealing—but do those who assault "deserve" to be assaulted?

How about those who murder?

How about those who rape?

In the case of student Salt, would such an action make you trust the university more? Would you feel comforted by the action taken by the dean?

Would a dean willing to take this action be legitimate in your eyes?

If we apply the same understanding to the legal system itself, it is possible to see that certain types of responses—if they are too brutal and too harsh—will simply horrify the general public to such a degree that people may turn on the state itself. It is reasonable to be irate about your home being burglarized and it is reasonable to want vengeance over the attack against your friend. But is it reasonable for *the state* to engage in acts that caused you so much emotional pain or could these acts diminish the credibility of the state itself? You may want your friend's killer to be executed—perhaps somewhere where all can witness the retaliation. But we must also consider how such a display would resonate with people in general. If you saw countless acts of retaliation against the human body on display (on your way to work or school), would that make you more likely to respect and admire the state or simply fear it?

If you fear the state then the contract has been greatly harmed, perhaps broken irrevocably and replaced by authoritarian threat. And if you become more like those you despise, if the state of which you are part reflects the behavior of the *traitor* then how is the state preferable, more honorable, reasonable, and just?

We cannot simply execute or exile our offenders because they no longer wish for our protections or our benefits. Doing so might at first seem expedient, even desirable, but ultimately it harms the state; when the state is brutal, we fear it and with fear comes loss of respect. In our eyes, the state loses legitimacy. But we do not think that it is naïve or inappropriate to suggest that a healthy state where the individual is powerful and instrumental, where one's life can be lived independent from the frivolous will of select persons, would be desirable for most, even those who have strayed. We believe it is perfectly possible, if not almost inevitable, that those who violate the rules of the club will continue to recognize the benefits of membership and will want to rejoin it when and if they are permitted to do so. The benefits are too great. But the benefits exist because we have invested in the contract and we abide by its rules. With some exceptions for egregious violations, we cannot permanently deny those who have broken the rules the chance to rejoin the club, to rejoin society. Doing so would mean transgressors have no way to regain the benefits of the collective and so have no incentive to try to rejoin it. Furthermore, denying transgressors the opportunity to rejoin the club will also likely make them despise the club, question its fairness, its legitimacy, perhaps despise its members. This does not suggest that we actually live in a world that lives up to this ideal. Power may be consolidated unfairly in our states and equal protection may be more of a dream than a reality. But it is only *ever* a reality within the structure itself. We are only able to achieve equal protection—and minimize suffering—within civilization itself, with a strong social compact.

This is only an opening discussion of punishment. A way in. It is important that we ask these questions in order to adopt a strategy that best serves our self and collective interests.

We return to how we specifically punish—and how we *should* punish—in Chapter 8. But as you walk away from this text today, consider the following question: are actions that harm the collective—that threaten the social order—more serious than actions that do not threaten the collective?

CHAPTER 4

MEDIA AND CRIME

> "Voters perceptions of crime continue to conflict with reality: Despite double-digit percentage decreases in U.S. violent and property crime rates since 2008, most voters say crime has gotten worse during that span" (Gramlich, 2016).

Most of us have the good fortune never to encounter direct criminal victimization—we are not, robbed, raped, or arson victims—and yet experience shows people hold very strong opinions about crime and how we *should* respond to it. It is not surprising people hold strong opinions about crime given the widely publicized harm and suffering it causes. What is surprising is that people hold such strong opinions absent direct personal experience or consideration of empirical evidence. Data examining opinions about the crime rate and criminal justice issues indicate Americans generally hold inaccurate beliefs (Swift, 2016). This chapter focuses on the role of mass media in shaping our thoughts about crime and justice. There are many media formats and the effects of mass media are complex. Some scholars even distinguish between "mass communication and the mass media ... Mass communication involves the use of the mass media—print media ... electronic media ... (and now the internet) to communicate with large numbers of people at the same time" (Berger, 2005, p. 117). For simplicity, we use the expression "mass media" to refer to communication "with large numbers of people at the same time." Although we occasionally refer to significant characteristics of a particular form, we do not distinguish between media formats although doing so is worthwhile. For example, reality TV shows are especially powerful in shaping beliefs as these take us to crime scenes and draw us in as if we are witnesses to events as they happen and are able to participate in solving crimes (Cavender & Bond-Maupin, 1993; Fishman & Cavender, 1998).

Mass media coverage of crime is ubiquitous and the content is largely homogenous with an emphasis on violent crimes–*the least common type of crime*. Even though the delivery medium changes, the song essentially remains the same. With many sources, apparently confirming "the facts" about crime it may seem unnecessary to question them; but to understand the impact of media upon our thinking about crime and justice we must do so. Since mass media tends to focus on violent crime, mass media often shapes our understanding of crime through *nontypical crime events*. Intense mass media focus on atrocities is especially influential and often generates calls for immediate (and sometimes drastic) responses (Kappeler & Potter, 2005). For example, the deliberate random shootings of schoolchildren and the subsequent media coverage serve to further fear and anger about crime. Of course, our outrage toward such atrocities is appropriate; the acts sicken us and raise questions about human nature. But as these events unfold, we get incomplete and often inaccurate information through mass media. And yet the initial coverage shapes our overall beliefs about crime and how we should respond to it. Such tragedies reveal a typically overlooked and significant factor: emotion. The tragedy of violent events should not be minimized, they enrage us; yet we must realize this rage narrows the focus of our responses to crime and leads to support for extremely punitive responses (Hartnagel & Templeton, 2012; Johnson, 2009). We contend that while anger about criminal atrocities is justified it should not serve as the basis for policies to deal with crime; anger limits the range of policies we consider and so will not necessarily produce the best response. Our anger may also lead to the severity of punishment warned of in Chapter 3; excessive punishment may delegitimize the state in the eyes of many. In essence, we allow our anger toward perpetrators to determine our response to criminal events. We believe that understanding mass media coverage of crime and justice is vital for understanding media effects upon our thinking and ultimately our responses to crime.

To be clear: our intention here is *not* to question the harm arising from crime. Our goal is to raise awareness of how mass media crime coverage shapes our beliefs in the absence of personal experience. Common beliefs about crimes and responses to them are greatly influenced by mass media crime portrayals (Griffin & Miller, 2008; Kappeler & Potter, 2005) and we believe media organizations present information about crimes leading to overly simplistic beliefs that prevent nuanced understanding and hinder development of effective crime policies. Raising awareness of how media influences opinions about crime is fundamental. If people understand media effects they will become more critical consumers and be less willing to uncritically accept media portrayals and their implications. We believe the role mass media play in (a) shaping beliefs about crime and (b) shaping beliefs about how we *should* react to crime are fundamental to understanding our justice system. In this chapter, we discuss a number of mass media characteristics that impact our thinking about crime. We hope our readers will become more aware of how mass media impact their thinking about crime. To begin examining media effects let's first consider the social construction of reality.

SOCIAL CONSTRUCTION OF REALITY

The social construction of reality is a complex and important process. Examining the process helps understand how people form their beliefs about crime and lays a foundation for thinking about mass media influence. To get through the day, we need to feel we understand the world around us and that we have a measure of control over it; we gather information and reach what we believe are informed conclusions that guide our actions. In many instances, our decisions are based upon assumptions we believe to be sound perhaps because experience supports them, or perhaps because they just appear to make sense based on the available information. Our decisions and beliefs are also generated through interaction with others both directly and indirectly. That is, we meet friends who give us information directly; and we also get information "indirectly," from people we do not know and/or from unknown origins–we check Facebook, we watch TV, we receive tweets, we listen to the radio, and we watch movies. When meeting with friends, we are typically unaware of factors influencing the information they give us. Ignoring the wide range of personal factors that might influence how information is exchanged (jealousy, boredom, etc.), it is likely much of the information we get from our acquaintances has come to them through mass media or through others who have themselves been informed to some extent by mass media. Indeed, a tremendous amount of all information we exchange is dependent upon mass media; and yet we are generally unaware of the extent to which that information is shaped by mass media. Our obsession with crime is not inevitable. The social construction process we describe recognizes there are many things with the potential to become social problems. From a marketplace of potential problems some rise to the top and are identified as legitimate and serious problems that deserve both our attention and our action. Others do not. This is the social construction of reality (Quinney, 1970; Surette, 2014). Issues become social problems in part because of their objective qualities and in part because we are frequently exposed to them in a variety of formats and settings that lend them the appearance of "greatest importance." In this way, crime is presented to us frequently and dramatically and so dominates as a significant social problem (of course, we do ***not*** suggest that crime is not a significant social problem; we are only stating that its prominence as a social problem is largely due to the massive media attention it attracts).

To further illustrate the social construction of reality, let's consider the following example of Walter Lippmann's (1930) island. On Lippmann's island in 1914, English, French, and German nationals live in apparent harmony, cut off from all outside sources of information. Each 60 days, a steamer arrives and the captain provides island residents with information about the outside world. In Lippmann's example, the captain informs the islanders of the outbreak of World War I and so the English, French, and German learn that:

> ... for over 6 weeks now those of them who were English and those of them who were French had been fighting on behalf of the sanctity of treaties against those of them who were Germans. For six strange weeks they had acted as if they were friends, when in fact they were enemies. (1930, p. 3).

There is much in this. The islanders had lived peacefully, harboring no ill will toward each other, but with this news they are faced with the decision of being members of "their group"—English, French, or German—and so the English and French might unite in opposition to the German, or they may remain "naïve" islanders who continue living in harmony. What Lippman demonstrates is once information is received, it has tremendous implications for the behavior of recipients. But there is an additional twist here, what if the captain delivering the information about World War I had for any number of possible reasons presented inaccurate information or in the most extreme instance simply made the information up. Would that have mattered in terms of the behavior of those receiving the information? To the extent recipients believe the captain is a credible source with no interest in misinforming them, it is likely the recipients will believe the information and begin the internal struggle of processing the information and deciding subsequent action. That is, to the extent the information is believed a *new* social reality with very real behavioral consequences is constructed that has significant potential to change island life.

Lippmann's example informs us in many ways. It brings to light the sociological maxim that "if men define situations as real they are real in their consequences" (Thomas & Thomas, 1928, p. 572). That is, the islanders *were* friends but now they have (a) new information with which to define their situation (regardless of the information's actual accuracy) and (b) that definition will affect the real relationship they have with fellow islanders. Of importance here is that nothing in the immediate surrounding has changed, all that has changed is the knowledge they have received. It is important to again emphasize the level of credibility information recipients assign the captain; if they think him a dishonest drunkard living aboard a ship to escape the realities of everyday life the information is likely harmless; if they respect him as the venerable master of a large sea faring vessel he and his information are more credible and more heavily weighed.

Lippmann's example also highlights what Merton (1948) describes as the self-fulfilling prophecy evidenced in the creation of "in-groups" and "out-groups." Living in ignorance upon the island, it seems there was little national group allegiance affecting relations between the English, French, and German citizens. However, the introduction of the information about World War I, without any material change in the island world, establishes that—contrary to what they thought—the friends were not actually friends. In this instance, the information highlights group differences; and to the extent individuals share a group identity that supersedes their daily relations, neighbors of different nationalities become English, French, and German first, and neighbors second. They avoid and ignore each other at best; attack each other at worst. And yet, through shared information, previously unrelated people (including strangers) unite as group members, and this larger group identity supersedes the existing everyday condition. Members of the "in group" are collectively "us" and those in "outgroups" are "them." To be clear, "they" are fundamentally different in ways we may or may not be able to clearly articulate; but "they" *are* different and therefore deserve to be treated differently from "us" (Merton, 1948).

Such is the situation with those who commit crimes. Both empirical work (Becker, 1963) and anecdote illustrate that those committing crimes are believed to be part of an out-group fundamentally different from "us"—the law abiding—and so deserve to be treated differently based upon the available evidence (Merton, 1948). In class, we often survey students about involvement in crime by (a) them *or* by (b) someone they know. Despite some variation, a dominant response pattern typically emerges: almost all of our students—or people our students know—commit crimes (some of them are quite serious: carrying a weapon to school, sexual assault, drug sales). But most of our students and the people they know were not caught; and if they were caught it is typically by parents who punish them *or* by police who refer them to parents. The point of this exercise is to indicate the false distinction between the "non-criminal-us" and the "criminal-them": the distinction is most often not based upon behavior but whether the behavior was discovered and how formal and informal actors reacted to the behavior. The falseness of this distinction is repeatedly lost however; throughout our courses those who commit crimes are typically referred to in derogatory terms indicating they are thought of as a fundamentally different group of "others." The empirical evidence supports this effect: most Americans report undiscovered and unpunished involvement in criminal behavior at some point in their life (Bohm, 1986; Shelden, Brown, Miller, & Fritzler, 2016); most Americans, therefore, do not become part of that segregated group of criminal "others" their behavior might warrant. This pattern is not mysterious when we examine how we form our beliefs about crime and offenders.

Using Lippmann's analogy we can see that absent direct experience with crime, we rely on external sources of information; we contend that mass media is the external source of information with the greatest potential to shape our beliefs about crime. If we accept the premise that mass media is the external source of information with the greatest effect upon our beliefs about crime, it is important to examine central characteristics of mass media and mass media content to understand how they impact our thinking. To understand the impact of media upon our beliefs we believe it is illustrative to consider traditional news media reporting as it draws attention to how media can misinform us while seemingly reporting only objective facts. There is also empirical evidence of the strength of news reporting upon how people think about crime (Gilliam & Iyengar, 2000).

NEWS REPORTING

The press has traditionally played an important watchdog function in our country's history (Calvert & Torres, 2011) with freedom of the press guaranteed under the First Amendment. Even though a free press suggests there is little government control or censorship it does not indicate that the press is free from external influence. In fact, because the press is not government owned and censored we may have an exaggerated sense of its "freedom" and this might make us especially susceptible to its influence without knowing it (Herman & Chomsky, 2002). When we believe the press is free, we have little reason to really scrutinize it, to question it. We may realize press sources adopt different perspectives in reporting, but we do not feel the need to question the content of the press, we are generally willing to believe the events presented to us and that these events constitute credible information.

We believe the first principle to understand when thinking about mass media, including news reporting, is that it is a for-profit business and so in the process of informing us about the world it must do so in a way that generates profit; this is done through advertising (Herman & Chomsky, 2002). This is perhaps best conceptualized by thinking about mass media as businesses that sell audiences to advertisers (Chomsky, 1997; McChesney, 2004). The larger the audiences, the more people are reached by commercials and so the more advertisers must pay to access these audiences. The larger an anticipated audience the more profit can be made. The best example of this phenomenon is the Super Bowl. The final game of the football season guarantees a huge audience where ads themselves are celebrated as newsworthy events (Blackburn, 2018). The size of the audience promised by the Super Bowl is shown by the cost of advertising (Tomkovick, Yelkur, & Christians, 2001). The Super Bowl only happens once a year and so other formats that promise significant audiences to sell advertisers are important. Mass media coverage of crime is one way to generate audiences. People are fascinated with crime and crime shows are extremely popular, both fictional and reality based. Once a popular crime show format is established, it is repeated because it attracts audiences. What attracts audiences is the unusual and so consumers are exposed consistently to those crimes that are factually *least common* but, absent alternative sources of information, appear to be the norm. When it comes to crime, official sources demonstrate violent crime is least common (Federal Bureau of Investigation [FBI], 2018) and yet violent crime is most emphasized in media (this is reflected by the common maxim "if it bleeds it leads").

REPORTING

As we mentioned earlier, there is a built in preference for the unusual in news crime reporting, especially violence; even though these horrific events do occur they are rare and do not present an accurate image of "typical crime." We do not deny that atypical crime may be the most tragic; our point is that if this is what news consumers are presented with they will fail to realize that these are exceptions and they will come to think of them as representative of crime in general and they will develop attitudes toward crime and crime control based on such rare occurrences. Walker's (2015) "wedding cake" model of crime illustrates this point.

In Walker's model, the cases at the top are those that happen least often but are either done by well-known people (celebrities) or are sufficiently abhorrent that they attract massive news media coverage. The cases at the top are outliers as far as crime goes yet they attract the most news media attention. In the second layer of cake are the serious violent offenses committed by lesser known individuals, but that are sufficiently unusual that they attract news media attention. As far as news coverage goes, the third and fourth levels of the model are scarcely relevant—they may attract some media attention, especially at the local level, but they do not attract sufficient news coverage to bring them to our attention as representing social problems. This model illustrates that news media informs us about the crimes that are least likely to happen and does so in such tremendous volume that people, regardless of location, come to view these as "proper"—or typical—crimes and begin to think of appropriate crime responses in terms of these events (Potter & Kappeler, 2006). The focus on sensational crime also contributes to the image of offenders as "others," fundamentally different from the rest of us and so lends support to extreme policies designed to deal with them. Again we do not deny the seriousness of these events, but argue they have a disproportionate impact upon how we think about crime, offenders, and how we respond to crime. In highly publicized crimes, the incidents are often random, victims and offenders are often strangers, and extreme violence is common. Although highly influential, these characteristics do not represent typical crime and so are not an appropriate bases for creating policies to deal with crime. While generating profit has a huge impact upon media crime coverage we can see by examining news reporting that the reporting *process* itself contributes to the distorted media image of crime.

POINT OF VIEW

News reporting is especially well positioned to impact beliefs of consumers because it focuses on real events so the process used in reporting is important. News reporters are faced with the challenge of producing information to fit the organizational demands of their employer. News organizations need to find stories quickly and they need stories that fit their publication schedule and format. The effect of this is that stories are necessarily short and cannot present the depth of detail necessary for a nuanced understanding of crime. Instead, reporters must get "the facts" as quickly as they can, condense them and present them for dissemination in as little time as possible. This leads to simplistic depictions of crime. In the process of gathering information about crime, reporters play a significant role in the social construction of reality by granting legitimacy to some perspectives over others. Because expediency typically demands reporters use the most easily available source of information, reporters typically rely on the police. Police often go out of their way to assist reporters and provide press briefings where they make information available. The reporter is no fool, she knows she needs information and to get it she must maintain good relations with police. What does this mean? One effect of the situation is that reporters will generally avoid significantly criticizing police (Herman & Chomsky, 2002) and report the information police gives them. There are many sources of information that could be used, but for expediency police trump all and so the police point of view is presented most frequently. Because the police are a recognized authority figure and because their point of view is repeatedly presented, police gain a sense of "ownership" over the crime problem (Surette, 2014): police become established as *the* legitimate source of information about crime; and reporters often reinforce the police perspective as the "correct" one. We are not questioning the motives or expertise of police or reporters here. Instead, we are drawing attention to the process in order to raise awareness of the reciprocal relationship between reporters and police. We do not question the police perspective. We are emphasizing that by privileging the police point of view, other perspectives receive less coverage and this gives the impression that there is only one legitimate point of view when it comes to thinking about crime. We must be aware that the point of view presented in mass media is typically that of police, but that to really understand crime we need to consider multiple factors. For example, we know that social factors (e.g., poverty, employment opportunities) impact behavior, and to understand crime we need to understand their effect. It is not the job of police to highlight the impact of these social factors, but near-exclusive reliance on police for crime information precludes discussion of these important factors in crime reporting. It should also be noted that when police appear in media they are doing their job—and part of that job is to reinforce their legitimacy and highlight the good work they are doing; again this is appropriate, we would not expect any organization to frequently question or undermine itself, but recognizing that police must advocate for themselves further illustrates the one-dimensional image we get about crime from reporting that is dependent on information from police.

NARRATIVE

We believe mass media contributes greatly to establishing dominant narratives that have powerful effects upon beliefs about crime and that we must examine narratives and their potential effects. Narratives serve an important function in daily life as they provide us with a degree of predictability that allows us to safely navigate our world. Narratives function to "fill in the blanks" for us, providing important guidance concerning how we should behave and feel in often unpredictable situations. Narratives provide information allowing prediction that guides our thoughts and actions; but it is important to realize that the information we get from narratives does not reflect objective reality, but it is an approximation of reality. Although they are important, when we fail to realize the impact of narratives upon us, when we fail to recognize that narratives are approximations of reality often offering false prediction, they can mislead us. The impact of narrative upon behavior has long been recognized (Carli, 2015). To illustrate the potential of narrative to shape our thinking we turn to nursery rhymes. Nursery rhymes deliver common and powerful narratives to us at a young age when we typically lack alternative information sources. Nursery rhymes teach us many things: we learn the characteristics of villains—that there is an unambiguous right and wrong—and we receive explanations for crime (Thomas, 2015). The power of the nursery rhyme narrative is that it is highly predictive and consistent. This is fine in fiction where wolves are bad, children taste good, and grandmothers live alone in forests. It is important to understand, however, that the messages being sent in these stories, even though told over and over, help shape how people think about the world but are at best oversimplifications.

Nursery rhymes and folk tales give us the causes of crime. In a nursery rhyme, the big bad wolf is often hungry and so the proximate cause of her villainy is clear: it is a rational decision to satisfy her hunger through ill deeds rather than through acceptable means. In this sense, the behavior is understandable and the explanations simple: crime results from choices and crime reveals bad actors. The nursery rhyme does not give us the details. It does not distinguish between wolves who have been loved and those who have not; it does not tell us if the villainous wolf has starving cubs or has been consistently harmed by an abusive partner; it does not tell us whether there is societal discrimination against wolves that might prevent her obtaining food through more socially acceptable means. In this sense, then, the narrative does an injustice to our understanding as it conveys a sense that we have the details necessary to understand what is going on; as Thomas (2015) writes:

> " ... in the kind of story world we find in classic folk tales [and mainstream cinema], there is a sense of an underlying morality in which heroism and villainy are equally uncomplicated, defined by the actions of the characters rather than by any psychological, social or economic factors causing them to behave as they do" (2015, p. 29).

The classic narrative typically locates the causes of crime in the actor, ignoring more complex explanations that consider causal factors external to that actor.

Nursery rhymes also provide powerful messages about who villains are: wolves are never good; chickens are never brave. Of course, in reality we do not often deal with wolves and chickens but the establishment of these groups as distinct and unambiguously good or bad has an important effect—it tells us wolves *in general* are bad and chickens *in general* are cowardly. To return to Merton (1948), nursery rhymes reinforce the concept that there are distinct groups in which members share common characteristics showing them to be similar to other group members and different from nongroup members. That is, nursery rhymes introduce us at the youngest possible age to the idea that there are distinct in-groups and out-groups that differ fundamentally; the group differences are not just physical (wolves are furry, chickens lay eggs), but established as part of the character or personality of the group members. In this sense, then all wolves are associated with villainy and chickens with cowardice because of *inherent* characteristics.

Because nursery rhyme narratives are consistent and we are widely exposed to them at a young age (and also as adults as we read nursery rhymes to children) they have great potential to impact our thinking about crime. When we come to think early in life that criminals share common distinguishing characteristics, that the causes of crime are rooted in individual characteristics and that there is an unambiguous right and wrong in all situations, the themes from nursery rhymes have considerable potential to shape our thinking about crime. Clearly, nursery rhymes are not solely responsible for the narratives we hold—they are one example of how media impacts us—but we extend our discussion of nursery rhymes into ideology. We propose nursery rhyme themes can form the basis for later ideological beliefs about good and bad, right and wrong, crime and justice. Ideology is powerful in thinking about crime and so we move from discussion of nursery rhymes as a foundation for ideology to discuss ideology directly.

IDEOLOGY

There are many ways to think about ideology and we present some ideas here to illustrate how we conceptualize ideology and its potential to impact thinking about crime and justice. Wales (2001) defines ideology as follows:

> "any system of values based on ideas or prejudices and cultural and social assumptions which amounts to a pervasive, unconscious, world-view" (2001, p. 196).

In this definition, ideology stems from widely held beliefs that exercise an *unconscious* impact upon how we view the world. This is important. To the extent that ideology is based upon commonly held beliefs and assumptions, we can see the relationship between ideology and narrative; to the extent that narrative draws upon "ideas or prejudices and cultural and social assumptions" it helps to shape the way people view their world and ensure the longevity of prejudices and assumptions. Especially significant is ideology's "unconscious" effect; because we are unaware of how ideology impacts our worldview we do not question it, we have a sense that what we think represents some sort of objective "accuracy" and as a result we often fail to question the information we receive, especially when we think the source is credible.

In a discussion of political ideologies and crime policies, Cullen and Gilbert (1982) define ideology, stating:

> ... ideologies tend to rest on sets of unexamined assumptions rather than upon solid empirical data, tend to have an emotional component, and are relatively resistant to change (1982, p. 36).

These authors present important characteristics of ideology. Ideology is inflexible, immutable: once a set of beliefs is accepted as accurate or "right" we do not quickly or often question its accuracy. Ideology involves "unexamined assumptions": when we accept a set of beliefs as accurate or right, we generally do so without serious examination of the assumptions on which the ideology is built. The characteristics of ideology allow us to continue to uncritically accept information we are presented with and at the same time reject that which we disagree with. Ideological beliefs are especially strong because they have been found to be self-fulfilling; for example, research illustrates the damaging role of "confirmation bias," where people actively seek out information that supports their ideological beliefs and simultaneously reject that which questions those beliefs (Nickerson, 1998). Cullen and Gilbert's definition also highlights the importance of emotional effects stemming from ideology. In nursery rhymes, and in typical mass media portrayals of crime, innocent victims are targeted by calculating villains. The observed injustice arouses anger, and anger reduces our capacity to evaluate information, especially when it is considered to be valid (Moons & Mackie, 2007). Returning to crime, we can see how anger calls for punitive responses. For example, Hartnagel & Templeton (2012), found a significant effect of anger about crime upon punitiveness: as self-reported anger among research subjects increased, so did their support for punitive responses to crime such as capital punishment and chain gangs for prisoners.

CRIME THEMES OR BLURRING THE LINES

It is also important to note that mass media coverage of crime often blurs the lines between distinct events, creating "crime themes" in which different offenses are placed into a single category increasing its perceived severity or prevalence. For example, in his analysis of news reporting Fishman (1978) describes a crime theme as a "unifying concept" that:

> ... presents a specific news event or a number of such events, in terms of some broader concept. For example, the mugging of an eighty-two year old Bronx woman can be reported as "the *latest instance* of the continuing trend in crimes against the elderly" (1978, p. 46).

In generating crime themes, then, reporters cast "disparate incidents" as examples of a single crime theme. Having established the "crimes against the elderly" theme, Fishman found subsequent offenses involving elderly victims (rape, murder) described as other instances of "crimes against the elderly." Such a general crime theme gives the impression that all crimes against the elderly are similar; but such generality obscures important differences that might provide a more nuanced understanding of crime involving the victimization of senior citizens.

The tragedy of mass shootings also illustrates creation of a crime theme. There is no recognized credible source of information about mass shootings but a number of sources offer information. One popular source is *Gun Violence Archive* (2018), which has been widely used in mass media to convey information about the number of mass shootings. Since *Gun Violence Archive* groups together fundamentally different activities into a single category of "mass shootings," it actually contributes to the establishment of mass shooting as a crime theme, or a single crime type (Cox & Rich, 2018). According to *Gun Violence Archive* methodology (and the FBI's definition) a "mass shooting" involves a single instance with four or more shooting deaths or injuries. The result is that extremely different incidents are placed together as mass shootings. For example, following this methodology, mass shootings can include significantly different (although tragic) events: a "school shooting" in which four or more people are killed or injured is classified as the *same type of crime event* as a "gang shooting" in which four or more people are killed or injured; and the "school shooting" and the "gang shooting" are both classified as *the same type of crime event as* a "bar brawl" that results in four or more people being killed or injured through gunfire in a parking lot outside a bar. The commonality in these incidents is the number of dead or injured and the use of firearms; beyond these factors the events are entirely dissimilar; placing them together as part of a single mass shooting theme or category of mass shooting serves to significantly exaggerate the numbers. Let's be clear: from a practical standpoint we are not going to develop effective policies to deal with school shootings by examining parking lot fights outside bars. And we do *not* deny the problem of gun violence. Our point here is that misleading data contributes to inaccurate conclusions, and our conclusions are what shape beliefs and attitudes, and shape how we think about crime and how we respond to crime.

Given the extent of media coverage, we find the mass shooting crime theme to be particularly important. For many, mass shootings are associated most strongly with atrocities at schools and colleges and these events understandably elicit powerful emotional reactions like fury. It is this fury along with the presentation of seemingly credible evidence that can lead to uncritical acceptance of the data and to belief in a greatly distorted image. Because they are uncommon, sensational crimes get massive media attention. We are frequently (and possibly inaccurately) informed about them. Make no mistake: these crimes *are* tragic and important; but to lump them together into a single crime theme is misleading. A simple medical analogy demonstrates the problem: no one would ever assume everything in the category of "body organs" is the same. While the heart and the spleen might be classified as "body organs" no one would argue that they are equivalent. So, it is with crime.

We hope this chapter has encouraged you to think more critically about how you come to know about crime and about the quality of the information you receive about crime. Given the impact media crime portrayals have upon our thinking about crime, it is vital consumers carefully assess the information they receive if we are to gain a better understanding of crime and develop better policies to address it.

CHAPTER 5

DETERRENCE AND CHOICE

This is a chapter on deterrence and rational choice. Although deterrence is discussed in many different parts of this text, this chapter specifically details the propositions, assumptions, and potential issues with deterrence models and with mapping choice perspectives.

Deterrence is appealing to people because it feels natural, sensible, appropriate: "we should scare people into law abiding behavior." If John does a terrible thing we should do a *worse* thing to John so that (a) John will never do it again and (b) John's friends–and other people who hear about John–won't ever even think to do what John did.

The model is fairly simple:

1. Raise the cost of crime through formal sanctions (arrest, conviction, incarceration)
2. Sanctions should be swift, and certain, and appropriately severe

Or:

1. As the ***severity*** of punishment for action (A) goes up → the likelihood of participation in action (A) goes down
2. As the ***swiftness*** of punishment for action (A) goes up → the likelihood of participation in action (A) goes down
3. As the ***certainty*** of punishment for action (A) goes up → the likelihood of participation in action (A) goes down

The deterrence model assumes that people who participate in crime are rational and that they are aware of the punishment—the punishment is known, transparent, even advertised. An illicit action becomes favorable if the cost for engaging in the action is minimal. But keep in mind, this only works if you are *aware* of the punishment. If you are *unaware* of the punishment, then it is difficult for the punishment itself to be the reason for your behavior. Transparency and knowledge are essential. Therefore, for punishment to have a deterrent effect, you have to have a sense as to punishment and the likelihood of arrest, conviction, or incarceration.

We think people may have a general romantic attachment to this approach because it seems to reflect who they are as people—they don't like pain, they run from things that hurt them (we tend to agree with disliking pain). So if Sam Smith hurts you, then you will be afraid of Sam Smith. The punishment must be something that either you are afraid of *or* something that you really do not like. Otherwise the sanction is not a cost.

Therefore, if we *raise* the cost of crime, we are *raising* that which is undesirable to the actor. But a word of caution, the deterrent effect is likely to be less powerful if:

1. The actor has always expected the punishment or cost (or the actor believes that the cost or punishment is in some way inevitable)
2. The actor has prepared for the cost (or the cost is insufficiently painful to the actor)

If either of the above overlapping conditions is met, the power of deterrence is greatly diminished.

Why is this point important? Because it is likely that sanctions will not be equally appreciated across populations. Therefore, if we limit our creativity within the criminal justice system—particularly in terms of available sanctions—then we are likely limiting the deterrent effect of those sanctions. Just because you are scared of prison does not mean that everyone is scared of prison. Just because you are scared of spiders, water, the dark, space, rats—does not mean that everyone is afraid of those things. Real punishment, from a deterrent perspective, would highlight that which the individual actor least appreciates (or fears, hates, runs from).

This is not to suggest a psychological exam in order to inflict the greatest amount of pain (like in George Orwell's, 1984); instead this requires a broader use of our creativity in order to employ deterrence to reap its greatest gain. If we begin to recognize that pain does not indicate torture or even a physical or mental attack—just as punishment does not automatically mean prison—then we begin to see that there are a thousand necessary duties and options *within* society that would adequately shape behavior positively because of the individual's dislike for them.

Deterrence usually works in two ways: specifically and generally. With **specific deterrence**, the state attempts to change the actor's behavior by punishing the actor himself. With **general deterrence**, the state attempts to change other peoples' behavior by punishing a select individual (e.g., make an example out of someone). We can execute people for murder so other people don't murder. This would be a form of general deterrence (of course, in practice, the best research tells us that there is no evidence that the death penalty *generally* deters). We can imprison you for 25 years so when you get out you don't repeat the act for which you were convicted. This would be specific deterrence.

We are not actually talking about policy here. This is a discussion about an actual deterrence model. If we subscribe to deterrence, then we need to understand the rational actor and apply the sanction appropriately to shape behavior. Beccaria (1764) believed that hard labor was a greater deterrent than the death penalty because the state could manipulate years to generate many levels or degrees of pain—pain felt by the actor and pain witnessed by the public.

Keep in mind: **incapacitation** differs from deterrence because it prevents behavior irregardless of actor choice. The person locked in a prison cell is incapacitated; she or he does not choose to reject crime; the choice to engage in crime (outside of her or his prison cell) is unavailable to her or him. The person who is executed is incapacitated; the dead do not choose to avoid crime or anything else. This distinction is important as deterrence is often presented as a rationale for certain forms of punishment, particularly execution; executing a person incapacitates them, it does not *specifically* deter them (although an argument may be made that executing someone may *generally* deter others from engaging in crime).

Deterrence assumes that people are rational. Rationality argues that people make decisions that maximize rewards and minimize costs. Said differently, we weigh the pros and cons of a particular course of action and choose that which benefits us most with the least cost. We will return to this in a moment. But it is important to remember that rationality is a core assumption of deterrence.

CHOICE

Deterrence and choice are therefore connected. Since deterrence is so appealing, choice must also be appealing and so we must consider choice. We do not intend to provide an exhaustive discussion of choice; this is an introduction and therefore our discussion reflects *one way to consider* choice in criminal participation.

Choice is pretty alluring—attractive and simple. We make choices all the time every day, so they seem simple. But are these choices simple? Is criminal participation actually simple? Is choice the real explanation for crime?

> *You made a choice to commit crime—nobody held a gun to your head;*
>
> *You were not forced to sell drugs—you made a choice;*
>
> *You made a choice to use drugs;*
>
> *You made a choice to rob the store.*

These are direct and seemingly reasonable claims demonstrating freedom of choice. You may even find them appealing explanations. So let's consider how useful these explanations are. When entertaining an explanation for criminal involvement, we could ask many questions but our general goal is to prevent and reduce crime so let's consider two related questions:

1. Does this explanation help us to *understand* criminal participation?
2. Does this understanding help us to *reduce* or *prevent* criminal participation?

How does choice fare in explaining and enhancing our understanding of crime? We must acknowledge that people do not make choices in a vacuum; people are not isolated from context when they make choices. Situational—and, yes, individual factors—impact choices. You can't make a choice that is not available or that you have never heard of (by definition it is not possible). For example:

> Even though Jenus Joseph had never heard of Amherst College—indeed had never been told about it, never read about it, never saw it, never knew anyone who knew it—he decided to apply.

This isn't Jenus deciding to apply to a college that he did not know *much* about, this is Jenus applying to a college that he did not know *existed*. In this scenario, Jenus would not even know to apply to Amherst College. Clearly then, choice is, to a degree, determined by where you are, when you are, and who you are.

Let's return to dealing entirely with crime choices. Our decision and your decision and our neighbors' decision to engage in criminal acts. To help with this discussion, you decide if there is a difference between the following two scenarios:

1. Jenus decides to attend the University of Michigan instead of Michigan State because he likes Ann Arbor more than East Lansing.

2. Jenus decides to sell cocaine because he cannot afford incidentals at college (you know, books ...).

Are these equivalent choices? In this first scenario, Jenus' life might not be that different were he to attend Michigan State. Presumably, he is still going to college and he will still graduate (most people graduate). Regardless of his selection of college, he likely will get a job and his life outcome will probably be very similar. He may make different friends, pursue different love interests, even major in something different. And we are not suggesting that choosing college is not important. For Jenus and for you, it is very important. But in terms of crime–and the likelihood of criminal participation–it is not nearly as important. Jenus is not making a choice of college versus not college. In the first scenario, he is simply choosing a specific college. In the second scenario, Jenus makes a choice to sell cocaine. He makes a choice not to get a job or flip burgers or sell ice cream or cut hair. He makes a choice to act against the legal code. And he finds the decision to engage in crime acceptable.

So ask yourself, is the *process* the same; is the *decision-making process* the same in each case, (A) and (B)?

Most would say yes. You weigh the pros and cons of any decision and then opt for the choice that maximizes your benefits and minimizes your costs. This is rational decision-making–weighing the pros and cons against one another. And it seems sensible, logical, and systematic. But here we must acknowledge that after you have weighed the pros and cons you select the choice with the greatest reward *to you*. Presumably, you are not acting in someone else's best interest (but this gets complicated). You have written a list of pros and cons that is entirely subjective and is only including "costs" and "benefits" that you have considered and that are important to you. Of course, you cannot consider every possible factor (in this way, some have insisted that human rationality is "bounded" because it is limited in how many factors it can actively consider while making a decision), but the factors you weigh in making your decision are yours. We might assume that we know what factors influence choices (e.g., people engage in crime for money), but do we really know this to be so? Do we really know why Jenus is prepared to risk his college education by choosing to sell cocaine rather than get a job?

A simple objective model, therefore, now seems fairly subjective.

Let's consider how risk impacts choice: different people have different perceptions of risk. Some people jump out of planes, base jump, or launch themselves off cliffs with ropes tied to their feet. Other people don't. Some people will not even travel on planes because of their perception of the risk associated with air travel. The point is that people may make choices based on cost and reward but these choices often depend on the person's perception of cost and reward. Yet, even though the factors that fill the model may vary dramatically from person to person the actual model itself will not. And we can outline the model with relative ease:

1. Expected **rewards** from alternate courses of legal and illegal action
2. Expected **costs** of these actions
3. Expectations as *subjectively* perceived by the actor.
   - *If the **subjective expected utility*** (benefit perceived by the actor) *of an illegal or legal act is greater than the **subjective expected utility** of the alternative, then the person will engage in illegal or legal acts*

This is known as the expected utility model (abridged and tailored to crime). For a long time, it was assumed—and in many places it is still assumed—that this is how people make decisions (since this is an introduction, this text does not cover more advanced models of decision-making, such as prospect theory). In this chapter, we are only looking at this model of choice because it helps to illuminate how difficult it is to *map* choice—or to understand (a) how choices are made and then (b) generalize those findings to an overall policy of crime prevention.

Right away we see potential issues with the expected utility model for helping us to understand criminal participation.

For example, how does the actor subjectively perceive rewards and costs? Is her or his perception due to who she or he is as an individual—*a priori, prior to experience*— or is her or his perception *a posteriori—after experience*? If family and school and friends (and general experiences) influence her decision-making, then her or his perception is being developed through experience, it is *a posteriori*. Experience shapes the context in which her decisions are made. Remember: we are not talking about whether or not she or he likes strawberry or vanilla ice cream. We are talking about crime choices and crime choices are unlike other choices—and unlike other preferences—because they include objective and codified costs that other choices do not. Every crime choice includes a formal sanction as a potential cost and so in theory actors are able to consider perceived cost. This indicates that the *perception* of the sanction is entirely relevant, even necessary, to understanding rational choice. If nobody gets arrested for stealing in *our* neighborhood, then *our perception* of the cost of stealing is dramatically reduced. On the flip side, if everyone in *your* neighborhood gets arrested for selling drugs and you still sell drugs, then *we may perceive* you as "irrational" because you do not appear to be acting in your best interest. You know that the cost associated with selling drugs is extremely high and yet you still sell drugs. We could reasonably infer that either the cost of getting arrested is not that high to you (perhaps likely) or the rewards from selling drugs are simply too high (again, maybe likely). However, if we accept these conditions, then *rational choice only operates adequately within a social context*. And we would need to understand those contexts adequately in order to understand how and why those choices were made. We also must consider whether or not acting against your best interest is actually acting irrationally. Our above model seems to suggest that it is.

But first let's return to this idea of *a priori* and *a posteriori*. Reconsider the following explanations for crime:

> *She sells drugs because she* ***chooses*** *to sell drugs*
>
> *She uses drugs because she* ***chooses*** *to use drugs.*
>
> *He* ***chose*** *to rob people; he was not forced to rob people*

You might gravitate toward these explanations, many do. But let us do so after we have acknowledged potential limitations in our thinking. The above explanations are actually "types of people" explanations. Are certain "types of people" more likely to participate in crime because of who they are—naturally, inherently, *a priori*—or are certain "types of people" more likely to participate in crime because of their experiences—environmental factors including physical and social contagions (an *a posteriori* perspective)?

This might not be immediately apparent. Let's try another example:

> *Sally likes to skydive and base jump and bungee jump. She likes the rush.*
>
> *John is afraid of heights and does not like activities that increase his heart rate.*

Suppose that Sally has a lower resting heart rate than John and actually needs the adrenalin activities to raise her heart rate to a level that John achieves by reading Shakespeare. Could we then acknowledge that Sally may be more disposed to criminal acts—acts that may inspire high activity in the autonomic nervous system? This explanation might explain some of the variation but keep in mind that if we adopt this perspective fully we are suggesting that those who participate in criminal activity are somehow different than those who do not and that this is largely determined by birth.

However, if we adopt the opposite perspective and suggest that crime rewards are largely gained through experience—*a posteriori*—then we are acknowledging that neighborhood, peers, parents, school, all potentially play a role in shaping who the individual is and how she or he considers cost and reward. If you are concerned about your mother's reaction then you are responding to a social force. If education is important (or unimportant) to you because that is how you were *raised*, then you are again responding to a social force. The world that you grew up in has provided your social context and that has shaped you and made you who you are.

Don't forget: this is simply a discussion of the types of things we need to *first* consider in explaining crime and then *prove*. These are central issues of choice—at least with the expected utility model of choice.

But perhaps the most important question is whether or not the model restricts choice.

We do not mean to get dark, macabre. But it is important to make this comment: we actually lose our independence if we abandon our ability to harm ourselves, act against our own self-interest. Our morality may insist that we not act but it cannot *prevent* us from *being able* to act. To illustrate the inherent shortcoming further, it may help to take the model to an extreme condition. This choice model seems to indicate that suicide can *never be* rational. There is no benefit that is greater than the cost associated with the loss of the actual actor. Indeed, what benefit *to the actor* is greater than the cost of her or his life (slow down: we are talking about "in the known world"—the only world we know)?

Presumably, you would agree that a "bad" choice is still a choice—perhaps regrettable, misguided even, but a choice. As human actors we do not ever have all the information and it appears to be a premeditated con to suggest that the model works when all the information is provided. If we assume that, we can infer your course of action when we truly understand your preferences then we not only eliminate "bad" choices; we also eliminate free will. But we think "bad" choices—choices that are not in your best interest—are still choices. And we think people frequently make "bad" choices.

To be clear, we can't quite see how the following small and simple decision is irrational:

> *You want to go to the bar even though you have an exam the following day. You deliberate, ponder, and then go to the bar with the intention of drinking heavily.*

I might judge this behavior as foolish, not a sensible choice. But not irrational. If we are serious with this inquiry we return to the same impasse. The expected utility model is limited in that it either promotes a type of person argument or a type of environment argument. I can reject the claim that adequate information will prove the model correct because under no circumstances would there be adequate or sufficient data or information to undermine the model. If we assume that people are making choices, we need to be able to map those choices, to model those choices. If we are unable to map choice, then it is not a theoretical explanation; it is an assumption of human behavior that *cannot be tested.* If the model cannot be tested, then it cannot be an explanation for crime. Theoretical explanations must be testable and falsifiable (otherwise they would provide little insight into human behavior beyond speculation, opinion, unspecified belief).

> **In brief**: if we cannot test "choice"—because we are unable to effectively design a model that explains choice—then choice is not an explanation for crime. It is an assumption on human behavior. Similar assumptions on behavior are that we are born good, or that we are born insatiable, or that we are born as blank slates. None of these assumptions is provable (or falsifiable) and therefore none of these assumptions is actually a theoretical explanation. They can *inform* explanations but they *cannot be* the explanation itself.

This all makes a simplistic understanding of choice rather problematic. It is particularly problematic for criminal participation and for offender-specific crime policy. If we believe that "choice" is an *explanation* for criminal participation, then we need to be able to construct a model that illustrates how choices are made. And we must expose that model to rigorous testing. All this points to recognition that explanations for choice must focus on the *a posteriori*, experience, and context as these are the only factors that can be exposed and subjected to testing; we are unable to know the *a priori*.

CHAPTER 6

REHABILITATION AND RESTORATION

This chapter examines rehabilitation and restoration in criminal justice. Rehabilitation is probably a familiar term; restoration has entered the justice system more recently. Much debate continues about the nature of restoration and its appropriate use. But both are important concepts with considerable bearing upon justice system goals; both deserve close examination. But before our examination begins, it is important to briefly comment on deterrence.

As discussed in Chapter 5 people often find deterrence to be an appealing punishment goal; pain *should* prevent people from engaging in crime. Beccaria first championed deterrence in *1764*: "(t)he end of punishment, therefore, is no other than to prevent the criminal from doing further injury to society, and to prevent others from committing the like offence ... " (Beccaria, 1764). When deterrence is the punishment goal we hope the pain of punishment prevents people from choosing crime in the future (specific deterrence); by making citizens aware of punishment practices we also hope they will avoid engaging in behaviors that result in punishment (general deterrence).

Deterrence is coercive; while it may have some positive impact upon behavior, evidence shows that it does not bring about significant reduction in crime (Paternoster, 2010) and there are potential downsides to its use. We *hope* the pain from punishment encourages people to avoid future behavior risking such pain; but we risk a number of undesired effects.

For example, the punished may feel they have been treated unjustly; as a result, they may turn against the punishing institution. And there are instances when deterrent practices, although painful, bring about their own rewards. Reputation for toughness is often important (Anderson, 1999) and toughness can be demonstrated by enduring punishment. In this case, continuing prohibited behavior is incentivized through efforts at deterrence; the punished person is admired for her or his willingness to be punished and her or his willingness to resist the institutions of punishment. And if we disproportionately punish certain people based on who they are, then this will challenge the practice of punishment: it will seem unjust. Resistance, therefore, to deterrent practices will be encouraged and even esteemed. With deterrence we attempt to change the rational calculus of those who have offended or of those who might offend. We want the official cost—generally recognized as arrest, conviction, or incarceration—associated with the offending behavior to be greater than the reward gained from the offense. Deterrence assumes that it is possible to make the individual *choose* not to offend because of the sanction attached to such action.

While deterrence seeks behavioral change through sanctions, the punishment goal of rehabilitation seeks behavioral change *by changing the individual*. In this chapter, we define rehabilitation as *efforts that provide individuals who have offended with realistic opportunities for legitimate behavior*; when deterrence is the goal of punishment even a person who fears punishment may risk prohibited behavior if they lack realistic alternative behavioral options (after all the behaviors may be fun and the risk of apprehension slight). When rehabilitation is the goal of punishment, prosocial behavior becomes possible and desirable, and clear efforts are made to allow those who have offended back into mainstream society. Remember from our discussion of justice in Chapter 2 that all other things being equal people want to be part of society.

Let's begin the rehabilitation discussion by putting crime into context and considering factors that might prejudice our thinking.

Because popular depictions of crime typically involve the least sympathetic offenders who commit violent crimes (Walker, 2015), we must recognize that such depictions contribute to fear of crime[1] and cause people to question the goals of rehabilitation or restoration (Callanan, 2005). We recognize that some offenses may be too abhorrent, some offenders too dangerous, to make rehabilitation or restoration seem relevant. But we also warn that focusing on outlier offenses generates outrage and anger that can blind us to the realities of crime. Failure to understand what crimes *typically* occur may harm important efforts that attempt to bring those who have offended back into society. When we acknowledge that the majority of crime is nonviolent and results from routine interactions; when we recognize *typical* crime, rehabilitation and restoration are more plausible. Let's take a closer look at rehabilitation.

WHY REHABILITATE?

Why should we even try to improve the lives of those who have violated the social contract and harmed fellow citizens? This question is important; it must be addressed if our efforts are to be sincere. An important objection to rehabilitation is that it poses unacceptable risk to society; tragic and widely publicized atrocities portraying rehabilitation as misguided are presented as exemplars of rehabilitation dangers and the justice system's inability to protect us from violent actors (Newburn, 2005). Such incidents should never be overlooked, but they are outliers that should not be taken as evidence that rehabilitation efforts are inherently flawed or unwarranted (an analogy would be abandoning train travel because occasionally some trains crash). In many instances, violent crimes could not have been prevented by the justice system. In others, the processes used to evaluate

1 For example in 2018 41.5% of Americans reported fear of being the victim of a random mass shooting (The Division on the Study of American Fears, 2018)

the dangerousness of offenders were either inadequate or used inappropriately (e.g., Altimari & Poitras, 2007). This is not to say there are no risks to rehabilitation; there are risks and some level of recidivism is probably inevitable; but we believe the risks from failing to implement *effective* rehabilitation strategies outweigh the risk associated with them. The key here is employing the appropriate empirical technique to determine what is effective and based on this premise:

> *Our argument for rehabilitation is that it is fundamental to community safety.*

With very few exceptions those who offend either remain in communities during their punishment or return to them following punishment. Here were refer mainly to returning prisoners but the points are also applicable to those punished in the commuity: without clear efforts to help returning prisoners choose prosocial behaviors and allow them back into mainstream society there is heightened risk of repeat crime. Recidivism rates are high: recently the Bureau of Justice Statistics reported that 83% of prisoners were rearrested within 9 years of release[2] (Alper, Durose, & Markman, 2018). This figure is remarkably high but should not be taken as evidence against rehabilitation. If we look at the pattern of arrests among parolees, we see that:

> "(f)orty-four percent of prisoners released in 2005 were arrested during the first year following release ... Sixteen percent of released prisoners were arrested for the first time during the second year after release, and 8% were arrested for the first time during the third year" (Alper et al., 2018, p. 5).

So 68% of prisoners are most likely arrested soon after release when they are in greatest need of efforts to help keep them

2 It should be noted that arrest does not mean new crime and is often due to parole violations.

from crime (e.g., assistance with housing, employment, transportation). Rather than interpreting the high recidivism rate as evidence rehabilitation does not work we believe these figures emphasize the need for implementing *effective* rehabilitation efforts and to make sure programming is available during incarceration and during the transition out of incarceration. Reducing recidivism through *effective* rehabilitation efforts will increase community safety. And if increasing community safety were not enough, effective rehabilitation efforts reduce costs in the long run. If those who offend do not change their ways, then they continue to engage in crime, to be pursued by police, to be processed through the courts possibly to be incarcerated; this sequence generates massive expense that exceeds the cost of effective rehabilitation efforts (Hoffman, 2017).

A BRIEF HISTORY OF REHABILITATION

Prior to the 19th century, confinement was rarely used as a sanction and rehabilitation was not the goal of punishment. Detainees were generally held as they awaited trial or as they awaited punishment. But during the 19th century, in an effort to "resocialize" those who violated the law, the penitentiary emerged as a place of punishment, a place of reformation. Those who were detained in the early penitentiaries were often isolated, living in silence, focusing on religious study. Although the term rehabilitation did not appear until the 20th century, early reformers considered the penitentiary as a place that would act as family, school, and church for the wayward individual. It was a place of reform; and this intention is very similar to our present understanding of rehabilitation (see Chapter 8 for a more extended discussion). And yet, by the early 1970s, policy in the United States largely abandoned rehabilitation as the goal of punishment and replaced it with a crime control approach (Cullen & Gilbert, 1982).

Just years earlier, in 1967, President Johnson had established the President's Commission on Law Enforcement and

Administration of Justice to review the U.S. justice system. Based on its findings the Commission published *The Challenge of Crime in a Free Society* in which it presented recommendations for criminal justice reform and reaffirmed the importance of rehabilitation. Concerning corrections the report stated:

> The prototype proposed here, if followed widely, would help shift the focus of correctional efforts from temporary banishment of offenders to a carefully devised combination of control and treatment. If supported by sufficiently flexible laws and policies, it would permit institutional restraint to be used only for as long as necessary, and in carefully graduated degree rather than as a relatively blind and inflexible process. (President's Commission on Law Enforcement and the Administration of Justice, 1967, p. 173).

Rehabilitation was clearly stressed in 1967. Through this approach, the justice system would maintain an individualized approach to dealing with those who offended. Ideally, each would be assessed in the system and a treatment plan developed. But despite the approach advocated in *The Challenge of Crime in a Free Society*, by 1974 the tide had turned; rehabilitation was rejected as a credible strategy for dealing with those who offended. The country quickly turned to the crime control model–focusing on deterrence and incapacitation (and sating demands for retribution).

Understanding the shift from rehabilitation to crime control over such a short period provides a valuable example of how our thinking about crime and reaction to crime can change and change quickly. Context is necessary to understand such rapid change in thought as it did not occur in isolation. During the 1960s and 1970s there was widespread social unrest: people campaigned for gender equality and civil rights; people staged mass protests against the Vietnam war; riots and bombings littered the front page of newspapers; a series of prominent leaders were assassinated (Martin Luther King, John F. Kennedy,

Robert Kennedy, to name a few); and violent crime increased substantially across the 1960s (see Cullen & Gilbert, 2013; Cullen & Jonson, 2011; MacKenzie, 2006; Pinker, 2013). In addition, there were also highly publicized acts of government violence against U.S. citizens. At Kent State University, Ohio, the Ohio National Guard generated massive public outcry in 1970 when it fired at students protesting against the Vietnam War killing four and injuring nine (Munves & Kelner, 2016). The public was also outraged in 1971 by unnecessary and excessive government violence at Attica Correctional Facility, New York, in response to a riot in which prison staff were taken hostage (Cullen & Jonson, 2011). And in 1971, President Nixon highlighted rising crime by focusing on illegal drugs: "America's public enemy number one in the United States is drug abuse. In order to fight and defeat this enemy, it is necessary to wage a new, all-out offensive" (Nixon, 1971). The cumulative effect of these events was a dramatic increase in the ***fear of crime*** (Liska, Lawrence, & Sanchirico, 1982) and a distrust of government.

The widespread social unrest and a rising crime rate led to questions about whether government could effectively control crime and whether the traditional focus on rehabilitation was still appropriate. Conditions were ripe then for the 1974 publication by Robert Martinson of *What Works? Questions and Answers About Prison Reform*. In his work, Martinson presents the findings of a review of existing offender rehabilitation programs stating that "(i)t is just possible that some of our treatment programs are working to some extent, but that our research is so bad that it is incapable of telling." He does goes on to state, however, that after examining over 200 studies the research provides:

> (v)ery little reason to hope that we have in fact found a sure way of reducing recidivism through rehabilitation. This is not to say that we found no instances of success or partial success; it is only to say that these instances have been isolated, producing no clear pattern to indicate the efficacy of any particular method of treatment (Martinson, 1974, p. 49).

It seems clear Martinson is cautiously rejecting existing empirical evidence as supporting the effectiveness of rehabilitation efforts; nevertheless, his conclusions were widely reported to provide scientific evidence that when it comes to offender rehabilitation "nothing works;" and despite subsequent efforts to clarify his findings—as well as a noteworthy 1975 publication systematically challenging his inferences and his results (Palmer, 1975)—Martinson's work provided a science-based catalyst for rejecting rehabilitation as a legitimate approach to dealing with those who offend; in the social climate of the time his work gave support to a new era of sanctions focusing instead on crime control.

CAN PRISONS REHABILITATE?

An important issue here is to really think about what we want prison to do (see Chapter 8 for a detailed discussion of prison). Currently, we often tolerate abhorrent prison conditions that are neither fair nor conducive to rehabilitation. The conditions are unfair because when the state punishes, a sentence is given and in the case of prison that sentence is removal from the rest of society for a time. Loss of freedom is the sentence: we prize freedom above all so its removal is a significant sanction. *The sentence is not removal from society plus exposure to degradation, fear, violence, malnutrition, and many of the other conditions common in our prisons* (McGuinn, 2018). Sentences are sanctioned by the state; no U.S. state formally sanctions brutal punishment—or torture—of those incarcerated. We argue that prisons can effectively contribute to rehabilitation, but if we want prisons to inflict pain on prisoners beyond loss of freedom, then this is *unauthorized and unconstitutional treatment* that can actually promote recidivism. Empicial evidence supports this claim (for example Harding, 2014). We believe exposure to punishment beyond the state imposed loss of freedom (in the form of abhorrent prison conditions) is likely to make prisoners further resentful and question the legitimacy of the punishing institution. To use the club analogy, would we want to gain membership to a club that had subjected us to ridicule and degradation? Or would we likely rebel against that club? For prisons to rehabilitate, they must be used only to carry out the sentence imposed by the state and they must prevent the emergence of conditions that constitute punishment beyond that imposed by the state.

Does Rehabilitation Punish?

Let's begin this discussion by considering how punishment is often perceived.

Perception One: We aren't tough enough on those we punish.

A common belief is that the justice system often does not really punish people: 45% of Americans continue to believe the justice system is not tough enough on crime (McCarthy, 2016), *and* may in fact treat those who offend better than they deserve (Cullen & Gilbert, 1982). Such perception is an obstacle to rehabilitation: if we do not believe people are really punished or punished significantly, then why be concerned with their rehabilitation?

Perception Two: We perceive prison to be the gold standard of punishment and anything else as not "real" punishment.

Both lines of thought reveal a focus on retribution rather than rehabilitation as the goal of punishment and fail to acknowledge the importance of rehabilitation so we address each here.

Perception One: We aren't tough enough on those we punish.

With this perception there is a failure to fully consider what constitutes "toughness" in punishment and we must do this. We believe toughness stems from a retributive desire to inflict pain on offenders. To move beyond the perception that those who offend are not adequately punished (and so the desire for retribution is sated) we must learn about the *costs* (or pains) of *rehabilitation efforts* required by the justice system. This is vital.

So are we "too soft" when we punish? It is useful to pause here for a moment and think about whether we would "feel punished" were we mandated to do some or all of the following: surrender part of our income to pay fines and court costs; spend our free time performing community service; surrender our driver's license; travel weekly (possibly by public transport) to an inconvenient location and provide a urine sample in front of a stranger; travel to participate in court-mandated drug counseling; abide by a curfew from 7 p.m. to 7 a.m.; no longer associate with many of our friends and family members. It is likely many of us would. It is also likely many would argue that even if we recognize these sanctions as punishment they do not go far enough in dealing with those who offend. To this latter point, we believe there is again an important perceptual problem. As discussed in Chapter 4, we are most often exposed to sensationally tragic, violent offenses, and it is not difficult to imagine that for such offenses the punishments described above may seem "too soft:" they likely are "too soft" for many offenses. But if we focus on *the most common crimes*, those that are not sensational and *happen most frequently* (larceny, drug use, motor vehicle theft) are such sanctions too soft?

Perception Two: We perceive prison to be the gold standard of punishment and anything else as not "real" punishment.

Punishment involves some form of sanction for proscribed behavior, some form of cost to the offender *and there must be a cost.* Excepting execution, incarceration incurs the greatest costs. But what about alternatives to incarceration? Alternatives to incarceration are hardly rewards–*they involve costs to the punished* whether in terms of money, time, or labor. These costs are part of freedoms people value and their removal should be recognized as punishment (as emphasized above). But to recognize "real" punishment as anything less than prison requires us to think about our ultimate goal here: rehabilitation. Prison is not conducive to rehabilitation as we define it (*efforts that provide individuals who have offended with realistic opportunities for legitimate behavior*). Incarceration involves loss of employment (if employed), time away from family, degradation, exposure to inherently antisocial environments; if we use recidivism rates we see prison does not rehabilitate. Prison may satisfy some through retribution; prison may protect us from some who are dangerous; prison may even remove people who greatly offend us; but if those released from incarceration are greatly disadvantaged by that very incarceration, then we can hardly claim that the typical prison experience is conducive to rehabilitation. And if we consider the goal of punishment to be rehabilitation (as we have defined it), then we must change how we think about what defines and what constitutes punishment.

The long-held belief of using prison to reform those who offend presents a significant perceptual challenge for rehabilitation. Because we think of incarceration as the gold standard of punishment we fail to realize that "alternative sanctions" are also punishment. Illescas and Frerich (2014) recognize this dilemma and state "an innovative challenge for the future could be to consider community sanctions as penalties in themselves, and not as mere proportional adjustments or changes to incarceration" (2014, p. 21). The point here is that if we are to recognize rehabilitation as a legitimate goal of the justice system we must change our perception and realize programs and treatments used to change peoples' behavior—even if not administered in prison and not exclusively designed to cause pain—constitute punishment by impinging on a person's liberty because they *require* participation. Changing who you are, who you've always been, is not easy, is in fact challenging, even painful *especially when you also have to face who you were and what you did*. Even though rehabilitative programming is intended to foster positive change in the life of those who have offended it does not change the fact that it is punishment.

In the case of prison then, a person is removed from society and the punitive aspect is clear, it fits with our traditional conception of what constitutes punishment (Clear, 2012). However, it is more difficult to perceive alternatives to prison as punishment unless we recognize how alternatives punish. We use a practice from our state of Connecticut to illustrate the punishment inherent in an alternative to prison program.

In Connecticut accelerated rehabilitation (AR) can be offered to those who are "charged with certain crimes or motor vehicle violations if the court believes that those defendants will probably not commit more crimes in the future" (State of Connecticut Judicial Branch, 2017). This is a diversionary program (an alternative sanction) designed to keep people accused of certain crimes out of the justice system by helping them address the causes of their behavior and avoid gaining a stigmatizing criminal record. To many, allowing those who break the law a chance to avoid full processing through the judicial system and a criminal record may not seem like punishment. From our perspective restrictions upon the liberty of AR participants and the demand that they change their behavior is punitive. If accepted into Connecticut's AR program a defendant must satisfy criteria that significantly restrict their freedom; participants must follow program conditions that:

> (m)ay include things like doing community service, paying restitution, taking part in a hate crimes diversion program, getting psychiatric or psychological counseling, getting alcohol and/or drug treatment, or taking part in an animal cruelty prevention and education program. Defendants taking part in AR must also agree to the tolling of the statute of limitations (to give the state more time to prosecute the case if the defendant does not successfully finish the program) and to waive (give up) the right to a speedy trial. If the defendant agrees to the conditions, the defendant will enter AR and be released to the supervision of CSSD for up to 2 years [i.e. probation]. CSSD will keep track of the defendant's progress during that time to make sure that the defendant is following the court's orders (State of Connecticut Judicial Branch, 2017).

The restrictions that an alternative sanction place upon an offender's freedom constitutes punishment *and* can be evaluated for effectiveness. Once we overcome the conceptual hurdle that alternatives to prison are not punishment, we are able to move beyond a belief that prison is necessary for punishing and consider what is most important in this chapter: effectiveness in rehabilitating those who offend. We can then ask these essential questions:

> Do those successfully completing this program commit less crime?
>
> Does empirical evidence indicate whether the program works?

If the evidence suggests a reduction in crime then the program is worth pursuing. If the evidence suggests no reduction in crime then the program needs to change (or possibly be abandoned). With an empirical approach we can make informed decisions. This is the heart of "evidence-based practices": the scientific method is used to collect and analyze data to reach credible solutions. Bizarrely, if we apply the evidence-based approach to evaluating the effectiveness of prison the data (recidivism rates) suggest it is massively unsuccessful. And yet we persist with it. Why would we be likely to persist with the above effort if evidence showed no change in peoples' behavior? What if we asked you to invest your own money in a program with a failure rate of close to, say, 70%—would you do it? If not, then why would you want the state investing, year after year, in prison "treatment" that fails at such a high rate? Why would you oppose alternatives to prison that are punitive and might work to rehabilitate?

Let us be clear: *rehabilitation is not an alternative to punishment, rehabilitation is a form of punishment and punishment is inherent in rehabilitation*; by definition rehabilitation requires impinging upon a person's liberty and whether dealt with in a prison or a community (as illustrated above) a person's liberty is reduced. *Punishment happens when we impinge on a person's liberty*. If we consider the values fundamental to our society, then we prize freedom above all else. Uninvited interventions in a person's freedom, those beyond normative requirements to stay in good standing with society, constitute punishment.

WHAT DOES IT MEAN TO REHABILITATE?

Rehabilitation can happen even without significant social structural changes. Addressing widespread issues of inequity is desirable in the *long term* but it is unlikely in the *short term*. A strict focus on structural change diverts us from more immediately attainable goals. One important (and we believe attainable) short-term goal is perceptual change: perceptual change is necessary if we are to seriously pursue rehabilitation. We believe people must perceive rehabilitative efforts as punishment because punishment is inherent in these efforts: there exists no credible argument to avoid rehabilitative efforts on the grounds that they do not punish.

The ultimate goal of rehabilitation is to help those who have broken the law through specific, targeted, programmatic efforts. But what constitutes *effective* rehabilitation? Is one "rehabilitated" only when one completely avoids illicit behavior? Is this the only acceptable goal? In thinking about what constitutes effective rehabilitation, we believe people tend to view it as a zero sum proposition: you either are rehabilitated or you are not. But rehabilitation is more nuanced.

Let's consider the following cases:

CASE ONE

After years of alcohol abuse Sally's alcohol dependence causes her to lose her job, her marriage falls apart and she loses custody of her children. Sally funds her drinking through theft and is eventually arrested after trying to sell a stolen iPad to a pawnbroker. Sally is convicted and sentenced to 2 years' probation with 12 months of mandated treatment for alcohol dependence. A condition of her probation is that she must use no alcohol; failure to meet this condition will cause her probation to be revoked and she will be incarcerated for 6 months.

> Question: What would effective rehabilitation for Sally look like?

By her second year on probation Sally is free from alcohol *dependence*. She has found a job and she has been granted access to her children. She does continue to drink socially (on weekends and holidays) and her probation officer knows she continues to drink. Sally's life has improved; she is no longer involved in crime. But she is not abstaining from alcohol.

> Question: Is Sally rehabilitated? Why or why not? Should Sally have her probation revoked? What are the potential effects of revoking/not revoking Sally's probation?

CASE TWO

Kristen is addicted to alcohol and to methamphetamine. Her dependence on these substances has prevented her from finding employment and has led to the dissolution of her marriage and the loss of her children. To support her habits she has engaged in burglary, theft, and prostitution. She is currently homeless and her addiction has led her parents and siblings to sever ties with her.

> Question: What would effective rehabilitation for Kristen look like?

Let's imagine that Kristen is eventually arrested for burglary. She goes to court. The judge decides Kristen's criminal activity stems from drug addiction and sentences her to 3 years' probation with random drug testing and mandatory enrolment in 12 months of community-based addiction treatment. She must be drug free for the entirety of her probation. Violation of the sentence will see her probation revoked and she will be incarcerated for 2 years. While on probation and following treatment for her drug addiction Kristen is able to find a place to live, a job, and she no longer engages in crime to buy drugs. She starts to believe she can reconnect with her children and family. She does, however, occasionally test positive for methamphetamine use during her probation visits.

Question: Is Kristen rehabilitated? Why or why not? Should Kristen have her probation revoked? What are the potential effects of revoking/not revoking Kristen's probation?

What should we do in these instances? Should we consider just the continued (but not devastating) drug use and conclude there has been no rehabilitation? Should we consider other factors?

CASE ONE

Clear Probation Violation?

Sally's use of alcohol clearly violated her terms of probation.

Therefore:

Without Context

End probation and incarcerate Sally for 6 months

With Context

Sally is no longer unemployed

She no longer steals to fund her drinking

She is beginning to reconnect with her children

CASE TWO

Clear Probation Violation?

Methamphetamine is illegal, Kristen's use of it is a crime and it clearly violates her terms of probation.

Therefore:

Without Context

End probation and incarceration Kristen for 2 years.

With Context

Kristen is no longer homeless

She is no longer engaged in prostitution, burglary, or theft

She is employed and with her income she *pays taxes and the cost of her drug treatment*

She is thinking about reuniting with her children and family

She continues to seek help for her substance abuse and testing shows only sporadic drug use

Does the continued drug use in each case indicate no rehabilitation? Do we only focus on the behavior or do we evaluate behavior within the context of a given case? The answer to these questions may be in the eye of the beholder: some may feel continued drug use means neither is rehabilitated; others may feel continued drug use is unfortunate, and must be sanctioned (perhaps with a fine or house arrest to further restrict freedom (additional punishment), and extended participation in drug treatment). As a result of treating each person's drug addiction, all other criminal behavior has stopped. Neither Sally nor Kristen is committed to a criminal lifestyle. They are significantly less criminal (in Sally's case the substance itself is not illegal) and each is causing significantly less harm to society; each is also contributing to society through work and as a taxpayer. Would it make sense to apply the letter of the law and incarcerate Sally or Kristen? If either is incarcerated she will lose her housing, her job, her support system. Through incarceration, both of these women will likely abandon hope of reuniting with their children or family, will no longer be able to attend treatment programs and upon release will have to seek housing and employment with no money (and with a gap in their resume that they must explain to potential employers). Incarceration will cost considerably more than having Sally or Kristen continue to undergo addiction treatment in the community. So what should we do in these instances?

We do not pretend responding to Sally or Kristen's continued drug use is straightforward. We must consider what is in the best interest of society overall. It is probably helpful to consider these cases as grey areas. Indeed, flexibility probably helps when we think about rehabilitation: it is not an either/or proposition. Cases may be similar but they are not the same. In terms of rehabilitation, each case should get the attention that the above cases have received. In addition, we must consider that mandated punishment (incarceration) might be more harmful than the crime it is meant to address. Cullen and Jonson (2011) offer a useful medical analogy for thinking about rehabilitation:

> If we were to draw a more appropriate medical analogy, it might be to the search for treatments for cancer. This search has made important advances, but it is still plagued by substantial failure rates and by the need for ongoing research to do better in saving patients' lives. In a similar manner, correctional interventions will invariably be beset by higher than desired recidivism rates and by the need for continuing experimentation in what really works to divert offenders from criminal conduct. However, in both cases—the treatment of cancer and of criminality—the standard of success is not high cure rates but rather doing better than alternative interventions that are available (2011, p. 304).

From this perspective the goal of rehabilitation is considered and assessed in relation to *other alternatives*—it may not provide the ideal outcome, but to the extent it *more effectively* reduces crime than alternatives *it should be used and improved*. Our goal here is not to promote a particular approach to rehabilitation but promote thinking about what realistically constitutes rehabilitation. We suggest a "one-size-fits-all" standard for rehabilitation is neither realistic nor appropriate.

RESTORATION

As we define it, rehabilitation requires *efforts that provide individuals who have offended with realistic opportunities for legitimate behavior*; these efforts must include changing how we think about and treat those who engage in crime. What words immediately come to your mind when asked to think about people who have broken the law? We frequently ask our students this question and they consistently reply with a string of stigmatizing adjectives: lazy, scumbag, dirty, liar, asshole. Such derogatory language serves to mark those who break the law as "other" (Merton, 1948). Those judged to be lawbreakers become different in our minds; in a sense, they become "broken." These adjectives reveal a master status ascribed to those who break the law: they are thought of first in these terms, not as brothers, sisters, sons, mothers. These attitudes are surprising as research reveals almost all U.S. citizens report engaging in crime at some point (e.g., Shelden, Brown, Miller, & Fritzler, 2016); clearly there is no "us and them," no fundamental difference between those who break the law and "the rest of us." Yet our language implies such difference. Without changing how we think about those who break the law there is little chance of effective rehabilitation. How likely would you be to respect those who reject you? Would you willingly adhere to their laws?

The power of language to stigmatize is such an obstacle to rehabilitation that official changes have been implemented in certain jurisdictions. The Government of Scotland, for example, encourages use of language that is "inclusive to people with convictions and victims of crime" and advocates the phrases "person with convictions" or "person with an offending history" rather than the more stigmatizing term "offender" or its many variations (The Scottish Government, 2016, p. 14). Returning to the social contract: if we identify some people as "not of us," fundamentally different, then they are unlikely to be welcome in our collective; and from the perspective of those who are stigmatized it is unlikely they will want to be part of the collective that clearly derides them.

Effective rehabilitation also requires change in how we treat those who break the law. Currently, we utilize a series of practices that amount to sanctions beyond those imposed by the state and that reduce the likelihood of effective rehabilitation. There are many examples. We stigmatize those who offend by making records of their misdeeds available to those with the greatest power to help them rejoin civil society. Take employers, for example, a typical job application will ask whether an applicant has ever been "convicted of a crime." This question identifies the applicant as "an offender" at the outset, often eliminating any chance of employment. But we can act to prevent this, we have already done so in some areas. Nationwide, 33 states and over 150 cities and counties have adopted what is widely known as "ban the box" on employment applications (no questions about criminal record are permitted) so that employers consider applicants qualifications first, free from the stigma of a conviction or arrest record (Avery & Hernandez, 2018). Similarly, housing is essential to those who have offended and yet we place obstacles that reduce chances of finding affordable accommodation. For example, Public Housing Agencies that supervise affordable rental accommodations may disqualify "applicants with a history of drug-related offenses, violent criminal history or crimes that *threaten health, safety or peaceful enjoyment of the property* (italics added)" (Affordable Housing Online, 2019). Such criteria are so broad that they can effectively deny housing to anyone with a criminal record. There are many additional examples of policies reinforcing that those who are officially sanctioned for offending are "different;" these policies are obstacles to effective rehabilitation: loss of the right to vote, ineligibility to work in many fields, loss of access to benefits (e.g., food stamps) to name a few (Pinard, 2010). These "collateral consequences" of conviction are so extensive and detrimental to rehabilitation that federal legislation has led to the creation of the *National Inventory of the Collateral Consequences of Conviction*, "an online searchable database that identifies and categorizes the statutes and regulations that impose collateral consequences in all 50 states, the federal system, and the District of Columbia, U.S. Virgin Islands, and Puerto Rico" (National Reentry Resource Center, 2019).

At this point, you may be wondering why these collateral consequences of conviction should concern you, after all they affect those who have wronged us, those who have broken the social contract. You may also be thinking these sanctions are necessary to protect us from those who pose us danger. This is a complex situation.

It is certainly true: we need protection from the dangerous and the actions of some so offend us that we wish to be separated from them. These goals can be achieved through prison and there are certainly people whose behavior demands imprisonment. But for those who have completed their state-imposed sanction (either in prison or the community) and who we hope are rehabilitated, how do we justify the collateral consequences of conviction? Do these constitute punishment beyond that imposed by the state? We ask you to consider if rather than making society safer these sanctions threaten us by hampering conditions necessary for effective rehabilitation. If those who have offended are constantly treated and reminded that they are "less than the rest of us" does this protect us or threaten our peace? Does placing obstacles along the path to joining conventional society make it likely those who have offended will want to be part of conventional society—does this protect us or threaten our peace? These reactions may be consistent with a desire for retribution but do they assist rehabilitation? Do they make our society better?

Braithwaite (1996) recognizes the importance of both language and action in dealing with those who offend. He warns that those who offend are "shamed" by their behavior and highlights the importance of reactions to them:

> (t)he societies that have the lowest crime rates are the societies that shame criminal conduct most effectively. There is an important difference between reintegrative shaming and stigmatization. While reintegrative shaming prevents crime, stigmatization is a kind of shaming that makes crime problems worse. Stigmatization is the kind of shaming that creates outcasts; it is disrespectful, humiliating. Stigmatization

> means treating criminals as evil people who have done evil acts. Reintegrative shaming means disapproving of the evil of the deed while treating the person as essentially good. Reintegrative shaming means strong disapproval of the act but doing so in a way that is respecting of the person. Once we understand this distinction, we can see why putting more police on the street can actually increase crime. More police can increase crime if they are systematically stigmatizing in the way they deal with citizens. More police can reduce crime if they are systematically reintegrative in the way they deal with citizens (1996, p. 12)

Labeling theorists have long warned of negative effects from reactions to behavior and to those who break the law (e.g., Lemert, 1951); Braithwaite's distinction between stigmatization and reintegrative shaming clearly articulates the importance of our reactions to those who offend. Reintegrative shaming as Braithwaite describes it is consistent with holding those who offend accountable for their behavior (punishing them) but emphasizes they should not be rejected; this approach is consistent with rehabilitation as we define it and allows for the possibility of behavioral change.

RESTORATIVE JUSTICE

Concern that reactions to crime might hinder prospects of rehabilitation has contributed to the emergence of restorative justice; this approach reconceptualizes crime and responses to it and offers crime victims an increased role in the justice process. Restorative justice, although a relatively recent development in our justice system is actually consistent with traditional justice practices:

> Restorative justice has been the dominant model of criminal justice throughout most of human history for perhaps all the world's peoples. A decisive move away

> from it came with the Norman Conquest of much of Europe at the end of the Dark Ages. Transforming crime into a matter of fealty to and felony against the king, instead of a wrong done to another person, was a central part of the monarch's program of domination of his people (Braithwaite, 2002, p. 5).

Prior to emergence of the monarchy, disputes were settled between parties directly involved; the crime victim was the person wronged, not the state; the victim played a direct role in dispute settlement. It has been argued that the emergence of the "state as victim" in our justice system actually removes the victim from the justice process and in doing so effectively "revictimizes" them as their needs often go unmet (Christie, 1977). Restorative justice is an approach to dealing with crime that brings the victim back into the justice process; it is victim centered. In fact, restorative justice recognizes all parties harmed by crime and whose needs must be met for effective rehabilitation; the approach involves steps to meet the needs of each party: to restore them as much as possible.

So what does restorative justice look like? Let's consider the definition of Howard Zehr (Zehr, 1985). Zehr highlights, as we have throughout this text, that there is no "correct" way to respond to crime and current practices are neither inevitable nor "correct." He notes that our:

> (d)efinition of crime and justice, as common-sensical as it may seem, is only one paradigm, only one possible way of looking at crime and at justice. We have been so dominated by our assumptions that we often assume it is the only way, or at least the only right way, to approach the issue. It is not. It is not the only possible model or paradigm of justice—not logically, not historically (1985, p. 438).

Zehr argues that the way we currently respond to crime is generally a failure. Significantly, Zehr's restorative justice approach first stresses how our system fails crime victims. Addressing the needs of crime victims is fundamental to restorative justice:

> Victims have many needs. They need chances to speak their feelings. They need to receive restitution. They need to experience justice: Victims need some kind of moral statement of their blamelessness, of who is at fault, that this thing should not have happened to them. They need answers to the questions that plague them. They need a restoration of power because the offender has taken power away from them (1985, p. 435).

Restorative justice also considers the treatment and needs of those who offend and, as our discussion above indicates, current practices fail to do this. Again you may be wondering why should we have such concern for those who offend? From the restorative justice perspective those who offend must be included in the justice process for effective rehabilitation. As Braithwaite describes, we must strongly disapprove of behavior but do so "in a way that is respective of the person." Restorative justice attempts to do this while holding those who offend more accountable for their actions than current practices:

> Judges often talk about accountability but what they usually mean is that when you do something wrong you must take your punishment. I want to suggest that real accountability means something quite different. Genuine accountability means, first of all, that when you offend, you need to understand and take responsibility for what you did. Offenders need to be encouraged to understand the real human consequences of their actions. But accountability has a second component as well: Offenders need to be encouraged to take responsibility for making things right, for righting the wrong. Understanding one's actions and taking responsibility for making things right—that is the real meaning of accountability. Unfortunately, though, our legal process does not

> encourage such accountability on the part of offenders (Zehr, 1985, p. 436).

There are a variety of approaches to restorative justice but all revolve around allowing the victim to confront the wrongdoer and allowing the wrongdoer the opportunity to take responsibility for her or his actions, and after doing so, being given a more realistic chance to join conventional society. Neither victims nor those who offend are coerced into participation but a restorative approach provides both opportunities to heal. For those who offend restorative justice differs from traditional rehabilitation efforts by allowing them to "repent, turn around, admit responsibility, take responsibility for making things right, change directions" (Zehr, 1985, p. 436).

Discussion of specific approaches to restorative justice goes beyond our goal here but we encourage you to search in your communities for restorative practices. Restorative justice is used in many countries and has gained popularity in the United States in response to a wide range of behaviors in very different settings (Van Wormer & Walker, 2013; Center for Justice and Reconciliation, 2019).

CHAPTER 7

POLICING

In this chapter, we ask these central questions: why do we want police and what do we want police to do?

The police is an institution that is permitted by the state to use coercive force. This is our explicit agreement: if actors do not conform to state-sanctioned rules police are authorized to compel conformity. Today we take both the form and fact of police for granted but to understand policing we must examine its history and development. Given prominent media attention to abhorrently violent crime it may see redundant to consider the existence and functions of police: we believe many perceive the role of police to be law enforcement and nothing else. Such a narrow view overlooks the variety of demands placed upon police and the range of skills necessary for effective policing. As with other institutions (e.g., prisons), there is nothing inevitable about our police and what they do. In fact, it might make sense to think about police as surprising rather than inevitable. The formation of police organizations grants some citizens the power to exert force against other citizens on behalf of the state; this is not a proposition easily subsumed in the principles of the early American republic. More to the point, in the early republic such an institution would probably be perceived as violating fundamental social principles; it would seem to reflect the very overreach of government that led to our first civil war (usually referred to as the Revolutionary War).

To the colonists—and to early citizens of the United States—protection *from* government corruption and overreach was essential to the survival of the republic. Allowing neighbors to be roaming extensions of the law would undermine the very fabric of the fragile nascent state. Indeed, our early expressions of state identity demonstrate that we were wary of government power.

Consider the Bill of Rights.

Ratified in December 1791, the Bill of Rights is famous for its emphasis on procedural protections—*or limits on government actors*. In fact, as this document shows, we established a series of protections *from* the government (and *from* government actors). For example (and the following lists are not intended to be exhaustive), this is why we emphasized the importance of:

Right to due process

Right to counsel

Right to a speedy trials

Right to confront witnesses

And we demanded, for example, that government agencies are as follows:

Prohibited from *unreasonable searches*

Prohibited from trying people twice for the same thing (*double jeopardy*)

Mandated to show *probable cause*

The Bill of Rights does not avoid substantive protections—notably the protections of speech; but, overwhelmingly, we adopted *procedural protections* in our Bill of Rights (see Stuntz, 2011, he lists 16 procedural protections in the Fourth, Fifth, and Sixth Amendments). When we read the Bill of Rights, we see concern for, perhaps even fear of, an overreaching government body that—absent strict limitations—would be able to invade privacy without cause, without transparency.

To reiterate, embedded in the Bill of Rights is the belief that individuals require protection *from* government. It is not surprising, therefore, that the idea of police would seem incompatible with our core positions on democracy and liberty. Police, after all, are often law enforcers. *They are ordinary citizens acting as an extension of government.* Police have the power to remove citizens—to arrest, detain, kill.

So how could an institution that would have clearly irked the founders develop in the first place and be so necessary to our current state?

Before we address this question, let's briefly revisit privacy. Indeed, we may not have the resolute obsession with privacy that the founders did. But context matters. The landscape has changed. Foreign and domestic threats in the modern world arguably have far more potential for devastating the core of our state. Weapons are more powerful and more dangerous. Protecting the public might require severe restrictions. Each of us, therefore, must ask ourselves the following questions:

> How much privacy would we be willing to give up in return for government protection?
>
> Is it more important to be protected *by* the government or *from* the government?

In answering the first question, we might not feel the passion of Patrick Henry in 1775 as he famously intoned: "*Give me liberty or give me death.*" But at what point would state control push us to act? We are often given justifications for government protections. And, yet, could we be pushed too far? For example:

> Governing officials declare *all* roadways closed because an automobile is used in a terrorist attack on a roadway
>
> Cell use is widely curtailed because a bomb was ignited *somewhere* by remote trigger on a mobile device

Perhaps you agree that aggressively curtailing activity in *public* spaces is occasionally necessary for public safety—roadways must be closed, cell towers must be shut down. But *all* roadways? *All* cell towers? And what if, instead of generally targeting an area, the police target *specific* cell phones, *specific* automobiles that they deem "suspicious"? Consider the following:

> Should the police have a *reasonable basis* for searching *your* car? For searching *you*?
>
> Should the police be required to obtain a warrant to search *your* house? To tap *your* phone? To read *your* emails?

If you answered yes to any of the above questions, you believe in privacy. And you agree with the Bill of Rights that tells us the police must obtain warrants and adhere to reasonable searches. You believe, in short, in the requirement of police to demonstrate probable cause. But what if the police claim that they must search your home because of an imminent terrorist attack? Do we allow this search without accountability or should the police be required to demonstrate the risk level *at some point* (before, during, or after the fact)?

Privacy is not *only* about keeping secrets—although we have a right to keep secrets. Privacy is also about protection from the government. If we give our neighbors the right to arrest—and to use coercive force—does that also give them the right to know whatever they would like to know about us? We may want privacy even if we are not engaged in illicit activity: we may want privacy protections because of medication we are taking, or because of our sexual orientation, or because of our eating or reading habits, or because of any of a number of simple idiosyncrasies. We may want privacy simply because it is our right to have a life that is not picked apart and viewed by the casual whim of our neighbors. In the world today, with social media and viral videos, we may think that privacy is that much more important.

If you recall our earlier discussions of the social contract, you will remember that we are, each of us, the government. We do not hand power over to a few people and ask for protection (unless we take a Hobbesian approach). We each give up a certain amount of freedom, we each sacrifice *equally*, and in doing so we form government, *our government*. But have we sacrificed privacy? In forming the state, have we willingly granted our neighbor the right to intrude on our personal matters? And has she granted us the same right?

The Bill of Rights is evidence that we do not grant our neighbor this right. Civil liberty is the freedom from arbitrary government interference. This is what we gain through the social contract; since each of us is "theoretically" the government, is the state, we do not have the right to interfere, *arbitrarily*, in each other's lives. Presumably, thereby, privacy is paramount. Your life is not our business *without reason*.

Ultimately, it is probably prudent to have a healthy cynicism of the actions of those in power *and* regulate their actions or behavior. This was essential in the founding of the republic: *checks* on power. In theory (and hopefully in practice) each body, each institution, is designed to be checked by another body; and the entire system is designed to be checked by the electorate. To state otherwise, we do not blindly trust our institutions; our doubt actually *allows* those same institutions to thrive.

We are probably right to be suspicious of the motives of our neighbors, of our leaders, of other people. Ironically, mistrust in the motives of individuals increases belief in the system because we demand transparency, accountability of all government actors. And agencies that have the power to use coercive force—the power to remove people from their homes, from the streets, from society—must not only have limits placed upon their use of force, but must be held accountable through external regulatory oversight in order to ensure that the will of the people is not violated or infringed. In the early days of the republic, we were wary of forming an institution with state-sanctioned coercive power because we saw first-hand the abuses of government overreach.

So why would we develop police?

In many ways, by the middle of the 19th century, we had little choice but to place greater faith in a state-sanctioned police to address the myriad problems that began to appear, particularly in our urban areas. In fact, it is easy to imagine that an institution that solves social problems and serves our needs might be perceived as benign; we are happy with the institution if we perceive it to serve our needs and so we might avoid the close scrutiny demanded by the founders. But it is important to reiterate that avoiding such scrutiny goes against our founding principles. This is a mistake we often make. Much as the judicial branch checks the legislative branch: any agency authorized to use coercive force needs to be regulated by an external body. This helps to alleviate the central concern of the founders: corrupt and overreaching government agencies. So if we were so wary of police-like institutions at the end of the 18th century why did they begin to appear midway through the 19th century?

The short answer is population explosion. During the 19th century, the population in the United States increased dramatically. Captivated by "the land of opportunity"—the American Dream—many people made their way to the United States. The story of the United States has always been a story of immigration. We are a nation of immigrants. But people weren't just immigrating *into* the United States in the 19th century, people were migrating *throughout* the United States—from the south to the north, from the east to the west. The 19th century was largely defined by physical and material mobility. Large numbers of people migrated to cities and migrated out west; some saw great gains in wealth; others saw great losses of fortune (Friedman, 1993).

With such profound mobility comes anonymity, erasing of informal social control, the inability of the old social forces—family, school, church—to contain and mold the fabric of the modern state. Urban areas were filled with diverse populations that often lacked a consensus on social norms, on appropriate behavior. Neighbors often did not speak the same languages, practice the same religion, or embrace similar cultural practice.

In part, the disorder and the inability to communicate, to come together and solve local problems, helped fuel a breakdown in the social order. As a result of these breakdowns, local authorities realized the need for a policing body to restore order. Our problems, particularly in the city, were real. But we were not a people that trusted the government. Therefore, an organized, uniformed, and centralized police force—such as that adopted by the English at the same time—would likely have been widely rejected by the American people. It would have been a brash display of government power. Therefore, early police patrolled their own neighborhoods; they were mere extensions of the overall guiding culture; they were "of the people"—they were *especially* "of the people they policed." Appointed by ward bosses, and therefore political in nature, police often had close relationships to those in political power. There were no essential qualifications to being police. Beyond crime, police were asked to address a variety of issues of disorder that were not being addressed in the city: garbage disposal, street lamp lighting, soup kitchens for the homeless. Yet, even though police institutions were now necessary in the new urban environments, an America that was wary of state power would not have immediately accepted an organized and uniformed extension of the state.

Early police were not a unified agency, they were autonomous bodies dispersed along neighborhood lines; and unlike today's police with a clear central headquarters (e.g. One Police Plaza), early police were decentralized. Local recruitment served to remind residents that police were also citizens; familiarity with local conditions helped them carry out duties the neighborhood wanted. But individual police officers were given wide discretion:

When to use force

Which citizens to arrest

Which crimes to enforce

But police during this period did little to assuage citizen concerns over their association with government. In the 19th century, officers were often recruited through personal relationships with political figures. There were no standard criteria or basic qualifications required. There were no mechanisms to guide the discretion individual officers exercised. This first era of policing is generally referred to as the **political era** of policing. Due to the proximity of the police to political figures and other entities of wealth and power, this era was also characterized by widespread corruption.

The strength of the political era was the integration of the police with the community. The weakness was the widespread corruption, disorganization, inefficiency, and discrimination toward outsiders.

PROFESSIONAL ERA TO THE COMMUNITY ERA (1930S–1970S)

By the early 1930s, evidence illustrated the crisis that police faced: corruption, low standards, poor communication, inadequate training, community distrust. August Vollmer (1933) is credited with the first call for professionalization of the police.

So how were police professionalized? An important part of the professionalization process involved establishing a clear definition of what tasks police should and shouldn't do. Police began to define themselves as crime fighters—law enforcement, agents of crime control. To be clear, police in the professional era began to refer to themselves as law enforcement. With this change, birthed in part because a professional force requires a clear objective, police became inexorably linked with a single function of policing. Indeed, this transformation was so significant that it is very likely most people today consider policing and law enforcement to be *synonymous.* But remember, law enforcement is only *one* of the tasks recognized by early police. And yet, by the middle of the 20th century, much of the work of past police became framed as nonpolice "social work"; indeed, the very community needs that had initially spawned police became a target of derision (this continues to the present day). The decentralization that had created chaos and allowed for widespread corruption was replaced with One Police Plaza central control, complete with a strict and formal hierarchy. Police schools opened; police were given uniforms; police were *detached* from neighborhoods and were no longer recruited locally; police became "unemotional" enforcers of the law, presumably unattached to anything but the law.

In addition, during the professional era, police largely abandoned foot patrol. Preventative–or random–patrol in squad cars began to be the primary role of the beat officer. The distance between community and police increased. Response time became a key metric of quality service.

But in the 1960s and 1970s, crime began to rise and the police were unable to address it. Studies such as the Kansas City Preventive Patrol Experiment began to appear that suggested random patrol did not prevent crime (Kelling, Pate, Dieckman, & Brown, 1974)–potential offenders were not scared by the unpredictability of police patrols. Response time became a target as well: since most crimes are discovery crimes (the victim returns home and finds her or his house burglarized) arriving to the scene as quickly as possible isn't all that important.

It began to become clear that the police did not prevent crime. And by the end of the 1970s, police started to take a hard look at their practices and a series of innovations began to appear over the next decades: community policing, broken windows, problem-oriented policing, hot spots policing, pulling levers policing, third-party policing, evidence-based policing, CompStat. Some of these innovations were revolutionary, others were simple rebranding of past practices. And each is worthy of investigation on its own. But perhaps the most essential point is that the police began to rerecognize the necessary role of the public. Indeed, the relationship with the public is key to the police's ability to effectively control crime and fulfill *other* police duties.

Keep in mind: old models do not die easily. Even though innovations began to dominate large urban police departments in the 1980s and 1990s, many police in the United States simply continued to proceed with the same practices and worldviews that governed the professional era. The creation of useful innovations does not necessarily result in their adoption (see Rogers, 2003).

DISORDER AND BROKEN WINDOWS

A key priority for early police was physical disorder. Most of the early departments were in the north–Boston, New York, Albany, Chicago, Baltimore. In the north, particularly in the northeast, police agencies were developed to handle the disorder that did not fall under the purview of an existing agency. But disorder is not without controversy–the very perspective of what constitutes disorder will vary from person to person, neighborhood to neighborhood. Let's start with two claims fundamental to our discussion:

1. Police do not define disorder
2. Police do not define crime

Police are often asked to maintain order; but they do not define disorder. Police generally investigate and solve crimes; but police do not define crime. But wait, do police define crime by *not* arresting someone who commits an illegal act? Isn't police discretion defining acceptable and unacceptable behavior? These are important questions. And enforcement strategies clearly matter. But do not forget that the definition of crime, the writing of laws, comes from the legislature.

Broken Windows Policing

The implementation of *Broken Windows* was not without controversy. But a discussion about *Broken Windows* is important because it demonstrates that (a) policing is about more than crime and (b) policing strategies can be derived from theory.

Most policing strategies are atheoretical (i.e., sending more police to crime hot spots does not help us to understand *why* those hot spots exist). Wilson and Kelling's famous 1982 Atlantic Monthly article on *Broken Windows* celebrated foot patrol and illustrated the essential role of the community in defending public space.

The central argument behind *Broken Windows* is that crime develops at places that have high levels of physical and social disorder. Physical disorder is generally defined by graffiti, boarded up buildings, litter, soiled drug needles, discarded drug vials. Social disorder is about people and the activity that they engage in that makes residents unsettled: public intoxication, vagrancy, loud noise.

But disorder *does not cause* crime in this model. Instead, the model suggests that disorder leads to fear. If you live in a neighborhood with high levels of disorder, then you might stay indoors as opposed to play in the park across from your house. Disorder—teenagers dealing drugs, graffiti lining boarded up buildings—might cause you to withdraw from public space because you are afraid. The *type* of disorder that Broken Windows is most interested in is the type that causes people to withdraw. Different neighborhoods likely have very different perspectives on what constitutes disorder. Therefore, to understand disorder, it is necessary for police to understand the norms of the neighborhood. Police, in essence, need to embed themselves into the neighborhood. Obviously, this is a challenge for any policing strategy because police are essentially targeting *different* behaviors in *different* neighborhoods. In order to understand normative neighborhood behaviors, foot patrol becomes essential: police need to understand the different needs and demands of the different neighborhoods they serve—they cannot achieve this level of communication through responsive policing in cars.

This also means that discretion becomes critical as well. **Discretion**: decision to act; decision not to act. Police make decisions to act *and decisions not to act*. This is an important concept. In general, the police act when something that shouldn't be happening is happening or something that should be happening isn't and something has to be done about it. The decision to act or not to act is determined by the police use of discretion. The police don't always use force. Often the threat of force is sufficient to compel someone to do something. Herein lies one potential issue within policing: if police systematically act or do not act based on characteristics of people or characteristics of a neighborhood, then police are not responding to *behavior*, they are acting on assumptions about *types of neighborhoods* or *types of people*—and this is *bias*. Laws restrict how police may act but discretion allows police to not act (even though the conditions may call for action).

To be clear, the decision to not act is the greatest use of police discretion. Therefore, how the police choose to adopt this form of discretion often comes with considerable controversy. Because the decision to not act is essential to discretion and to police work, the check on these decisions must be made by a regulating force *outside* the police agency. Since police are extensions of the *law*, no action by the police should be beyond transparent hearings, no action should be hidden from public oversight. The police serve the law; the legislature writes the law; the public elects the legislature.

Let's return to Broken Windows.

According to the Broken Windows model, in order to reinforce informal control mechanisms the police must accommodate the residents that impose those rules in different neighborhoods (that means living in the community, understanding the rules of the community, knowing the regulars); and yet the police exist to help regulate behavior—not necessarily to define what behavior is bad. Different members of different neighbors will define different things as disorder and it is essential for police action to *reflect these localized concerns*. As previously noted, police—by definition—do not sit well with the underlying principles of our republic; therefore, if police do not appear to be responsive to the potentially diverging local concerns of citizens, then it is unlikely that police will be uniformly embraced as an agency championing the best interests of all citizens. This is a really complicated and complex proposition—one that challenges many of the practices that emerged in the professional era of policing. And this proposition clearly asks for more than strict law enforcement. The needs in neighborhood X may be different than the needs in neighborhood Z; if police do not recognize these disparate needs, then the perception of police by these neighborhoods is likely to be harmed.

Here is the general hypothesis of Broken Windows:

> Disorder goes untreated →
>
> Citizens become fearful and withdraw →
>
> Informal social control decreases →
>
> Crime and disorder increase

Because this is a complex model that challenges many of the assumptions of the professional era of policing, serious issues with Broken Windows do often appear during implementation—or *how* the police choose to adopt the innovation. For example, if police decide to define disorder as low-level crime and to enforce or restrict those behaviors aggressively and *equally* across all neighborhoods, then the police are not actually adopting a broken windows strategy—they are not acknowledging *localized* concerns; instead, they are adopting a *zero tolerance strategy*. And even if the model is adopted appropriately, there are real concerns about this strategy encouraging the targeting of "undesirables"—for example, homeless men and women (or other marginalized populations).

We make no claims about the merits of Broken Windows Policing. We include this discussion in our text because it highlights the complexity of policing and *the importance of the community in developing and defending public space*. We do recognize that implementation of this policing strategy has often resulted in a more aggressive form of law enforcement *at the cost of community building and community partnership*.

POLICE TOOL KIT AND LEGITIMACY

Police actors do not get to decide what should and should not be law— even if they are afforded a degree of discretion. This might seem to be contradictory but it is actually a way to understand that the police have options beyond arrest. Examples of police options include:

Submit formal or informal warnings

Provide diversion to alternative programs, agencies

Contact and work closely with community partners

Engage the family, parents

Provide general mediation

If we limit the police tool kit to *only* coercive power—even if they are able to employ coercive power—we do a great disservice. And remember: the employment of police measures should be based on *behavior* and not on identifying characteristics.

Let us return to crime definitions. So who defines crime?

The legislature defines crime and the punishment for crime (**substantive law**)

The legislature also defines the process under which criminal justice actors must abide (**procedural law**)

Remember: the legislature is not without restrictions. The constitution clearly defines certain substantive rights and clearly restricts procedure (recall the Bill of Rights). Therefore, unconstitutional laws are challenged and overturned by the courts. This is a check on the legislature.

We are not suggesting that law in action (substantive rational law) is the same as law on the books (formal rational law). It is clearly not the same and the practice of law enforcement is one cluttered by high demands requiring nuance. The courts are designed to review police action and often *reasonably* allow for exceptions on behavior. But remember, the police do not define what is and is not acceptable behavior.

It might help to consider the police as an extension of the rule of law *from* the constitution and *from* the legislature *to* the streets. This is one way to understand intention. This does not mean that adoption and implementation—or everyday practice—are without serious concerns, problems, and injustice. But wanting police to do better is not the same as not wanting police at all. Before we address the second claim, make sure that the first claim has to do with the intention and the purpose of the agency and not simply with its general practice (there are those who believe that police are beyond repair; there are also those who believe that the police are beyond reproach).

But the central question is, do we want an agency to have the authority to use coercive power? Do we want an agency to be able to arrest and detain?

If we do not want the police at all, then we do not want an agency to have state-sanctioned authority to use coercive power. This is a perfectly reasonable perspective. And we respectfully disagree. We believe that it is in our best interest to have an institution that is able to forcibly remove those who refuse to live by our laws, who disrupt our ability to enjoy public spaces, who intimidate and harm the fabric of our society. In short, we believe that police are essential to a free society. But we do not believe that police should be able to conduct themselves in a manner that places them beyond our legal codes, or that allows them to intimidate and harm local populations. We want police to be better; we want police to be regulated by an external governing body. To reiterate, the police should not be concerned about an external oversight committee if they are *only* acting within the law. And, as we have stated above, we believe that we all should be wary and even suspicious of government agencies; therefore, we should demand transparency, accountability. This is why we are so clear about the need for protection *from* government in the Bill of Rights, in our constitution, in our governing documents.

These claims do not render police useless; moreover, these claims do not allow citizens to engage in any behavior that harms no one else.

From the start, police were asked and focused much of their attention on maintaining the **status quo**. We asked, and we continue to ask, the police to maintain the status quo because that preserves the existing state. This is not a political statement. Instead, it is recognition that maintaining order is not the same as defining order.

Consider the following related and guiding questions:

1. If the status quo reflects the current rule of law, then should the police be obligated to enforce the status quo?
2. Is it the job of the police to "oppress" that which the existing law "oppresses"?
3. Should police agencies and actors acting outside the stated rules of government determine their own form of justice?

We are not promoting misuse of power by police agencies or actors. State actors clearly are able to abuse their power. But changing the status quo, altering the structure of the state, adjusting resource allocation, providing more for those who have less are necessary functions of healthy and thriving states but it is not the job of the police to be those agents. It is the job of the members of legislatures, of the general public. We ask the police to maintain the status quo because that preserves the *existing state*.

We should be clear: aggressively policing certain neighborhoods *because of* who lives there is not maintaining the status quo: it is an abuse of power. Detaining people momentarily or for significant amounts of time because of how they look, or how they are dressed, or how they are walking, or where they live *is not reasonable* and *is an abuse of power*. If police think geographically, they damage their reputation and the public's perception of the police. Maintaining the status quo is about enforcing existing law and allowing legal activity to flourish and dominate within *all* neighborhoods; it is not about acting on *implicit bias* or writing off entire neighborhoods, entire populations. Again: if police think geographically—or think in terms of an individual's group membership—they are not serving the public.

And yet you ask: what if crime is disproportionately occurring in certain areas? Shouldn't police consider those places as more "dangerous" and therefore shouldn't the police think geographically? Police obviously need to recognize the variation in crime events across a geographical area. Some areas do have more crime than other areas. Some areas have a lot more crime than other areas. The issue is not the recognition that certain places need more *services*, more police *assistance*; the issue is when police profile people because they live in areas that need more police assistance. Instead of assuming that areas of high crime are primarily filled with people who engage in crime (which isn't true), it is far more appropriate to recognize that the need in areas of high crime is higher and that people in those areas require more support, more help in dealing with crime. If police start with the understanding that *most people don't like crime*, they are more likely to recognize the simple fallacy in a geographical approach. We admit this can be a very challenging proposition.

But let us ask the questions that need asking:

A. If select laws are systematically biased toward certain groups of people then should the police enforce those laws?

B. What responsibility do police have to be agents of moral authority—beyond the letter of the law?

What should be clear is that an institution that is highly decentralized, has few if any consistent hiring criteria or qualifications, is unlikely to produce officers who are able to address the complexity of rule enforcement—particularly since discretion is an integral component to police work (and the decision not to act is the most significant form of discretion in policing).

So far, we have neglected to address bias—particularly in terms of processing. Are people treated differently by the police because of who they are (**differential processing**) or because of how much crime they commit (**differential involvement**). We have neglected this discussion not because we do not believe that it is warranted or necessary but because the purpose of this text is to understand the necessary and appropriate role of police and not the unnecessary and inappropriate harmful actions of police agencies. This is to say: if certain populations are treated differently by the police because of who they are then this is *an egregious* ***misuse*** *of police power*. This is, in our view, police misconduct. And it also prevents the police from doing their job. If police target certain people because of who they are they reduce community trust and institutional legitimacy.

> At this point, we would like to add an important note: police departments that developed out of slave patrols in the antebellum south and continued to operate on a model of white supremacy before, during and after the Civil War completely undermine the institution of policing itself; any police body that promotes a racial hierarchy is an oppressive, immoral, and shameful institution. We have not specifically highlighted the development of police institutions in the antebellum south because their very model cannot protect and cannot serve all the people of this country. They represent a policing model that we categorically reject.

To return to our discussion: if the community does not trust the police will the police be able to make the community safer? Will the public automatically trust the police if they arrest more people?

Why is the answer probably "no" to both these questions?

The general premise of legitimacy is whether or not we *perceive* the police to operate fairly. Of course, this perception might be dramatically different from neighborhood to neighborhood. *Perception,* fortunately or unfortunately, matters. In the age of social media, it might not matter if it is fair or unfair for a community to have favorable or unfavorable perspectives of police. But is it a necessity for police to understand neighborhood perspective in order to adequately police (protect, solve crimes, reduce disorder, etc.)?

This all means that police must care about more things than crime rates. The perception that the local community has about police actions and about the institution itself is essential for police to be able to do their work.

But remember, fair doesn't necessarily indicate equal. As an example, if your child required extra attention in math/reading/science because of developmental delays or other complications, then should all students receive the same extra attention (or if some children show up to school hungry because their family is not able to provide breakfast, should all students receive breakfast)?

It is also important to remember that this is not about taking sides. Bluntly stated it is not a question of being "for" or "against" police and pointing to specific events to support a given side, quite the contrary. This is a mistake often made. We are not offering a perspective that asks you to be either "pro" or "anti" police, the process that we ask you to undergo aims to address our overall guiding questions: why do we want police and what do we want police to do?

CHAPTER 8

PRISON

This chapter examines our use of prison in the United States. We neither support nor condemn the use of prison; but we encourage you to remember prison is not inevitable; like all other aspects of our response to crime, imprisonment is the result of state decisions. Keep in mind that prison and jail are not the same thing. Even though both are a form of incarceration, jails are primarily for those awaiting sentencing or those given relatively short sentences. In addition, jails are generally county run and operated, while prisons are state run and operated (the federal government also runs and operates prisons; but the vast majority of men and women in prison are in state facilities). In this chapter, we focus on prison specifically. When we use the terms incarceration and imprisonment we are speaking specifically about those sentenced to prison.

Prison is a fierce reaction to law breaking. It is worth remembering that imprisonment should not be considered lightly. When we imprison we physically remove men and women from society and forcibly confine them in detention centers. Although we frequently employ imprisonment as a form of punishment, it is not trivial.

So how and why did we decide imprisonment is a necessary response to crime and that prisons should take their current form? This chapter seeks to answer these questions; this chapter also introduces complications that arise when we choose such a form of punishment.

THINKING ABOUT PRISON

If we were to ask you why we use prison in this country—and use prison so liberally—you might respond with the following:

> We imprison to exact vengeance—it is revenge for what *they* did (**retribution**)
>
> We imprison to improve people, make *them* better (**rehabilitation**)
>
> We imprison so that *they* will not do it again and so others will not do what *they* did (**deterrence**)
>
> We imprison because *they* are too dangerous to be left on the street (**incapacitation**)

These responses—and there may be many other similar responses—are revealing. Language is important here. The use of impersonal pronouns allows us to ignore the human dimension of imprisonment: the imprisoned become *different* from the rest of us; we do not need to offer them the consideration we give to those we know or associate with. The responses also reveal an astonishing range of tasks that we require one institution to accomplish. Do we believe that prison can meet all of these goals of punishment? Do we believe imprisonment can meet all of these punishment goals *simultaneously*? Can we achieve retribution and rehabilitation *at the same time*? Does prison need to be able to meet all these goals of punishment? Does the public really demand—individually or as a collective—that each goal of punishment is met?

We might not all agree on the goal of punishment but do we, as a collective, demand all four? In short:

> Johnny might want vengeance (retribution)
>
> Sally might want programming (rehabilitation)
>
> Mary Lee might want to make an example of people (deterrence)
>
> Alexander might want to get rid of the "bad" people (incapacitation)

But can prison please all these people? Will any of them be displeased if prison is ineffectual or makes people "worse"? Is it reasonable to even consider whether imprisonment makes people worse when at the very least imprisonment has protected us from "them" for a time? These are important questions; but remember prison is not a philosophical proposal; it is an actual *state-run* institution.

Therefore, should the state be required to empirically prove the effectiveness of its own institutions? Should the state be concerned about outcomes for those who leave incarceration? As a parallel, should schools be responsible for student outcomes after they graduate? Using medicine as an analogy, would we accept medical practices without empirical evidence of their effectiveness?

Perhaps, most succinctly, should state decisions rely on public perception—and assumption—or on proven empirical evidence?

DETERRING OR AGGRAVATING?

Deterrence is appealing to many people because it seems to make so much sense: raise the cost of crime and people will not engage in crime (see Chapter 5 for a lengthier discussion on the propositions). Through deterrence, we can shape your behavior because of your fear of punishment (specific deterrence) and we can shape your peers' behavior because of how we punish you (general deterrence).

Or, in short order:

> If the punishment is really harsh then Bob Murderer won't murder. But Bob Murderer will murder if the punishment isn't harsh enough. *And* if Bob Murderer murders even with a harsh punishment attached then that punishment *isn't really* harsh or at least *not harsh enough* (the same approach applies generally: if you perceive Bob Murderer's punishment for murder to be adequately terrifying you will not murder).

Deterrence usually refers to formal sanctions: arrest, conviction, incarceration. It believes that an action by the state reduces criminal participation (of course, the actor must be aware of such a sanction, or the likelihood that the sanction will occur, or she or he is not being *deterred* by such a sanction). Swift, certain, and appropriately severe sanctions reduce crime—according to deterrence theory.

But are sanctions appreciated similarly across populations and does this matter? Is prison or the threat of prison appreciated the same by all individual actors? If Paul Prison expects to end up in prison at some point in his life, is it plausible that Paul Prison will, in some way, prepare for prison and that will mitigate the impact of prison?

Preparation aside, let's continue on this track a bit: suppose you believe that Paul Prison is not sufficiently *deterred* by prison because prison is not harsh enough.

So, you decide to make prison worse, harsher—more brutal. And you decide what you mean by harsher, more brutal:

> What type of amenities should be available?
>
> Should she or he have access to resources?
>
> Should she or he have access to family?
>
> > Access to activities?
> >
> > Access to programming?

Now put Paul Prison in this harsh environment for 10 years. What might happen? There are many possible outcomes (Paul Prison may die, get religion, escape); but from the many possible outcomes consider the following:

> Do you think Paul Prison will *get used* to this environment or learn to *survive* in this environment?
>
> Do you believe that she or he will transform from someone who engages in crime to someone who is now a law-abiding person?

Think also about *why* this outcome will arise. *Why* might the prison experience become something Paul Prison gets used to? *Why* might the prison experience transform Paul Prison into a model citizen?

We rarely hear people claim that they want prison to make people worse; but when we start to consider what prison might accomplish and why, it is easy to imagine that for many people prison may well contribute to making them worse. High recidivism rates (see below) suggest that at *best* prison is generally not improving people, or at least it is not preparing them to succeed upon their return to society.

But, let's return to responsibility for a moment. If the state physically removes men and women and places them in state run and operated facilities, then whose responsibility is it to prove that these same institutions work? Remember: the state is using tax payer dollars to operate these institutions.

THE RESPONSIBILITY OF THE STATE

If the state is making people worse *through its own punishment practices*, then it is likely failing to "correct"—moreover, if prison is allowing people to maintain current antisocial tendencies, then it is also likely failing to "correct" those men and women who are under its supervision. In each case, the prison institution is presumably "allowing" illicit behavior to continue among those who are under its care.

The state runs and operates prisons; therefore, we believe that the onus is on the state to *prove* that prisons "work." But also consider the following facts: as of this publication, the United States spends an estimated $80,000,000,000 on corrections annually (this is our tax money); close to 70% of those released will re-offend within 3 years; and the recidivism rate has not really changed that much in a very long time (Wagner and Rabuy, 2017).

Would you continue to invest in a company with this type of success rate? Would you send your child to a school with a graduation rate of 30%?

We believe a number of conditions must be met if we are to justify imprisonment. We also believe that the state should empirically demonstrate that these conditions are met.

Condition One: Prison should not make people worse *and to this end* prison should not allow people to continue to engage in illicit activity.

The second point extends to safety and security in prison. If we forcibly remove men and women from our streets because they have engaged in behavior that we do not deem acceptable, then it seems to be our responsibility to ensure that those same men and women do not engage in that same behavior while incarcerated in a state or federal facility. It also stands to reason that no employee be allowed to engage in behavior that violates condition one. This also leads us to condition two.

Condition Two: Loss of liberty is the punishment; those incarcerated *should not suffer beyond the loss of liberty*.

This is often referred to as the **keeper philosophy**. Loss of liberty, *incarceration*, is the punishment meted out by the courts. That is the sentence. We are not asked to nor are we permitted to add physical or mental anguish to this loss of liberty while incarcerated. It is not the role of staff to ensure that additional pain is felt while incarcerated.

Incarceration is the pain.

These two conditions highlight the importance of safety and security for those who live and work inside prisons (and jails). And safety and security are reasonable priorities for prison management. If we build prisons–if we build centers to forcibly confine men and women–then escape undermines the very purpose of the institution itself. If we ask people to work in prison, then it is reasonable for us to prioritize their safety, their well-being. After all, men and women voluntarily (with pay of course) enter prisons every day and act as officers, counselors, clinicians, teachers, nurses. We must protect these workers–*who choose to work inside*; we also intend to protect the public–*the body that chose to build and fund prisons*. But what about those who are forcibly confined, who are in prison against their will? Should they be protected from abuse–from physical and sexual assault?

It is not unusual for students to suggest that prisons need to be horrifying, terrible, brutal places; beyond the clear lack of evidence that brutality actually makes people better (and probably makes them much worse off), should we use the prison itself, a state built and operated institution, to scare our fellow citizens?

This is the exact premise of *Scared Straight* programs. In these programs, youth who are disproportionately at risk for future incarceration enter prisons and are presented with shocking and terrifying stories of prison abuse and prison violence. The stories of prison atrocities are told in person by the *actual* victimizers. As John DiIulio (1991) lamented:

> there is not a shred of evidence that the program [Scared Straight] reduces criminality among its teen participants; and, in part as a reward for their services in the program, several "lecturers" have been paroled only to commit new crimes and return to custody. But even if the program "worked," it would still be a fitting monument to the new penology as the underlying intellectual justification for a situation in which, without any sense of personal shame, professional embarrassment, or dereliction of public duty, government **officials rely on prisoners to "scare" potential clients with the officials' own failure to protect and guide–to govern–those in state custody.** (1991, p. 78 *bold added*)

The unsettling tactics of *Scared Straight* imply an inability for the state to run a state institution. Instead of actively "governing" the detained population–providing pathways out of crime (since close to 95% of those incarcerated will be eventually released) prison managers are in essence using those who have quarreled with the law–and perhaps quarreled rather seriously–to provide the necessary "guidance."

It is an odd proposition: threaten assault in order to dissuade people from assaulting.

To be blunt, this represents an openly inept and insecure state admission ("we cannot manage our institutions; we cannot keep incarcerated men and women safe"). But since there are many types of behaviors that can result in prison sentences but considerably less variation in the types of prisons available the assumption is that conditions arising from unmanageable institutions (e.g., physical and sexual assault) are warranted retribution for *all types of crimes*. We firmly believe that loss of liberty is *the* punishment and that all additional forms of punishment while detained—including but not limited to brutality—delegitimize the prison itself and are inappropriate and generally inhumane. Remember: this is not only about those who are imprisoned; if we make the institution inhumane, we are also subjecting prison workers to an impossible and dangerous work environment.

IS PRISON A SILVER BULLET?

Ask yourself the following questions:

1. Do you believe that people who go to prison leave prison "better"?
   This is an important question because it unveils our assumptions about the prison experience *and* it is actually an empirical question. We can define "better" in a variety of ways—less likely to commit crime, more involved as parents, less likely to use drugs and alcohol, more likely to maintain employment (to name a few)—and then we can measure outcomes across the population. We can answer this question. And this also leads us to a second related question:
2. Do you believe that all people who go to prison need the *same* thing—the same programming, the same treatment, the same services—in order to be "better"?

In order to answer this, consider the following four people who all enter prison after being convicted of second-degree robbery:

Billy has a serious drug addiction

Sally has a fourth-grade reading level

Jack has a history of conduct disorder and suffers from poor anger management

Jill has been shot five times over the course of her life

Should the prison—and hence prison management—treat all of these individuals as like cases? After all, each of the above individuals was convicted of the same crime. But for a variety of reasons, we might begin to ask ourselves why we are using one institution to solve potentially different types of problems.

But let's add another layer. Even if you believe the above cases should be treated *the same* do you believe that the above individuals will respond to prison in the *same way?* If you do not believe that they will respond to prison in the same way, is this problematic?

In question form (a form of summation of the above scenario):

1. Should all incarcerated men and women be treated alike?
2. Do people respond differently to the same experience?
3. Does the context surrounding the *reason* for crime A matter—or does it only matter that an individual committed crime A?

The first question asks us to consider whether or not a similar prison experience is appropriate for all incarcerated men and women: should all incarcerated men and women have the same experience or do individual differences warrant different experiences for different individuals? The second question asks us to consider whether or not people *respond differently* to the same experience. For example, would each incarcerated individual experience prison in the same way? Suppose we demand that prison must scare people. *Will it scare all people in the same way?* If we believe in deterrence we are primarily concerned about effectively raising the cost of crime so that the individual does not recommit (or commit for the first time) acts that are punishable by law. Deterrence does not require prison but it does require that the cost associated with an undesired behavior is greater than the reward gained by such a behavior.

But it would probably make sense for that cost to be specific to the individual. *Some* people are afraid of spiders; *some* people don't like the dark; *some* people are afraid of prison.

If you subscribe to rehabilitative efforts, you will probably arrive at a similar place. Different people require different services in order to successfully reenter society. Billy and Jack *require* different services because they have different *needs*. Sally and Jill require different services because they too have different *needs*. No matter how much we scare them it seems unlikely these people will be able to avoid repeating old behavioral patterns unless their *needs* are met.

Perhaps unsurprisingly, incapacitative efforts would also require individualized treatment. Different people who participate in crime have different criminal career lengths. Therefore, from an incapacitation perspective the goal would be to determine when people—based on a variety of factors such as age of onset, frequency of offenses—are no longer active in crime. Sentences, under this goal of punishment, would be tailored to the specific individual's criminal career.

Why is all this important? Because if we take each goal of punishment in isolation, it appears that individual-specialized treatment is necessary if we care about the actual success of the particular punishment goal. Using the goal of deterrence, how do we know what might deter Jack and how can we know whether the same will scare Sally? This calls into question uniform treatment—namely prison—for a variety of populations.

> *So now reconsider the third question: do you think the context surrounding the reason for criminal participation is important?*

Naturally, this all leads us to a central question about criminal justice practice:

> Do we demand justice practices that empirically demonstrate—*prove*—that they reduce criminal participation or do we demand practices that work *within* the prison?

Said differently, it might be worth asking if it is more important to you for us to adopt strategies that are proven to reduce criminal participation *regardless of the setting for these strategies* or is it more important to you that we find the best strategies that can be offered *within the prison environment*. Our punishment goals do not *require* prison; why are we so wedded to a practice that appears to be so limited in its ability to handle diverse needs?

And why did we even adopt the prison as punishment in the first place?

PRISON IN THE UNITED STATES

Although it is our intention to walk through the birth of the prison as punishment in the United States in a general sense, it is important to begin this conversation by recognizing that U.S. incarceration practices have disproportionately targeted select populations:

> [Our] policies have not impacted citizens of the United States equally. The likelihood of imprisonment is far greater for the uneducated and for people of color. Recent estimates suggest that close to 70% of black men who failed to complete high school spent one year in prison by the time they reached their mid-30s (Pettit, 2012). The disproportionate number of urban, poor, black males in prison suggests that mass incarceration may be more adequately described as "hyper incarceration" (Wacquant, 2010; see also Sampson & Loeffler, 2010). Sampson and Loeffler (2010) further demonstrate that, irrespective of crime rate, neighborhood disadvantage substantially drives incarceration rates (McGuinn, 2014).

This recognition of "who" is likely to be punished—particularly if "who" is more aligned with group membership and less aligned strictly with behavior—asks us to own our current morality (and seek to transform it if we see fit). Every age asks and answers the question of appropriate and inappropriate behavior (see Friedman, 1993):

What is it ok for people to do and what is it not ok for people to do?

This question is not always answered in similar fashion. Indeed, at the time of the first colonies, much of the unifying culture was focused on religion and organized through the patriarchy. Although the colonists brought English customs with them—particularly in regard to the criminal justice system—*living* in the colonies was not like living in England:

> Dominating forces of the king and the church hierarchy were not present
>
> Colonies were isolated, requiring a great deal of self-sufficiency and therefore requiring full labor participation in order to survive
>
> Winters, particularly in the North, were difficult
>
> Soil, again in the North, was rocky making clearing farm land difficult
>
> Local populations were already living in the Americas—often creating conflict, confrontation

God was at the center of the colonies—but this was not necessarily appreciated in the same way. For example, Massachusetts was overwhelmingly Puritan, Pennsylvania overwhelmingly Quaker. From the beginning, the law that was developed in the colonies—although heavily borrowed from the English system—primarily protected White men. And the main concern was the offense to god as this was a direct offense to society itself. An offense toward society *threatened* society.

In short order:

> Sin = Crime
>
> Crime = Sin

Therefore:

> Cause of crime = Sin
>
> Goal of punishment = Bring the sinner back into the community
>
> Method of punishment = Shaming

Most colonists would repent and confess and would be allowed back into the colony after a shaming ritual, a whipping (and/or fines). In rare occasions, the colonists did employ the death penalty and banishment. But the overall goal was to bring the wayward man or woman back into the fold. With small intimate communities, such as the communities in the colonies, shaming was effective.

> For example: if you were put in the pillory or in the stocks and your entire family paraded by you then it is likely this humiliation (shame) would have an impact on you and, potentially, shape your future behavior (similar to deterrence, the likelihood that you would repeat the act that warranted the pillory in the first place is probably greatly reduced).

But in a colony with few people and with high labor demands (including necessary and continual protection from nature's wrath) incarceration as punishment would make little sense. Why would the colony agree to lock Billy in Joan's basement—*and feed him*—as punishment? Not only would they lose Billy's labor but they would also still have to provide for him. The prison, therefore, was not rejected by the colonists; instead, it was probably never actually considered (Friedman, 1993). This point is essential. Each period asks itself why people commit crimes and then devises a strategy to address crime based on that explanation. Consider the following framework:

> The history of criminal justice is not only the history of the forms of rewards and punishments; it is also a story about the dominant morality, and hence a history of power (Friedman, 1993, p. 10).

For us today, therefore, it is important to continue to look at who we punish and to actively concern ourselves with our own morality. As we turn to the birth of the prison, keep this in mind:

> [T]he past and the present illustrate their (potentially divergent) morality through criminal law and therefore they likely used the prison to achieve divergent outcomes. The larger and more pertinent issue here is that the

> rationale for excessively high incarceration rates of today should be reconciled with our current morality. Either these rates reflect our moral position and therefore may remain; or they challenge our moral position and therefore must change (McGuinn, 2014).

To reiterate, every period asks: Why do we have crime? And every period answers the crime question through action (or inaction). The colonists' believed crime was sin; the colonists employed shaming techniques to bring people back in. This is similar to **reintegrative shaming** as discussed in Chapter 6.

By the late 18th century, the population in the colonies began to explode. Indeed, across the 19th century, a great number of people were moving into and across the North American continent. Migration and immigration were defining characteristics of the time period. As the population exploded, the influence of the key socializing forces began to lose power. Culture was no longer the key restraining force. In particular, the family, the school, and the church were no longer as effective at socialization (Rothman, 1995).

By the 19th century, legislatures began to target more conventional crimes, in particular crimes against property. Awarding strict penalties for "victimless" crimes (adultery, fornication) fell out of favor; strict religious explanations for criminal participation also lost ground. The failure of key social institutions became a much more appealing and prominent explanation for criminal participation.

At the same time, "Enlightenment" thinking continued to plant ideas of rationality, rule of law (as opposed to rule of man), equality, and individualism, onto the cultural landscape of a new country that cherished its newfound freedom and that believed itself to be a beacon of freedom. To many, and vitally, America was truly the land of opportunity and *freedom*.

If those who lived in America or chose to immigrate to America believed in opportunity *through* freedom, what would be the ultimate punishment for those who violated her laws?

Consider the following (late 18th century, early 19th century):

> Cause of crime: poor socialization (failing sway of school, church, family)
>
> Goal of punishment: *provide* that socialization (“*correct*” *them!*)
>
> Cultural reality: rationality, individualism, freedom
>
> Method of punishment ... ?

Out of this reality, grew the idea of designating a place of punishment where those who offended could be held and serve their penance (hence: penitentiary!). God was still central; but the needed reform was isolation and exclusion; society itself was ineffectively socializing. Therefore, remove people from society and place them in an institution that will “socialize” them.

> *Note: there is indeed irony in a society claiming that it is unable to socialize and therefore it must build new institutions to provide that “socialization” but does not challenge the very framework of the state itself that is likely causing that lack of socialization (the “freedom” so adored and sought by countless migrants).*

In 1790, the Walnut Street Jail, operated and conceived by Pennsylvania Quakers, opened a new wing called the “Penitentiary House” to hold those who had offended in isolation so that they may reflect on the wrongs that they had committed. In essence, this was the birth of the prison as punishment. A place where those incarcerated could read the bible, live in isolation, engage in solitary labor, and *become* reformed. The larger version of the Quaker Model, Eastern State Penitentiary, would open in 1829.

Around the same time, in 1816, the Auburn model was born in New York state. Although silence and reflection were also prioritized in Auburn, the model was work-focused and those incarcerated at Auburn were expected to work together, in silence, during the day and sleep in isolation at night. The men at Auburn made goods—generally out of supplies provided by private industry—and in the early years of the penitentiary period, prison labor began to be seen as a way to produce revenue for the state. The intention was to make the prison self-sufficient; but the "free" labor of the prison also allowed the institution to compete for contracts at much lower cost threatening economic competition.

From the beginning, there were market forces involved in prison practices.

Regardless of the different approaches, prison itself was appealing to policy makers and to the public. Odd as it may sound today, prison seemed to be a more humane form of punishment. Juries were more likely to convict; there was a sense that prison could reform, provide the needed guidance and socialization that was lacking in the *individual's* life.

But due to the overall appeal, by the late-19th-century prisons were overcrowded, disordered, and even though reform existed in the rhetoric of punishment prisons were largely brutal, undisciplined warehouses. Indeed, in these overpopulated and understaffed places complete with feeble discipline, there was little evidence that the institutions were able to deter or reform.

But prisons were not abandoned. Instead, reformers in the late 19th century believed that the issue was with inadequate prison governance rather than with the prison itself. In 1870, the National Prison Association published their Declaration of Principles.

Their main fix? **Indeterminate sentencing** practices.

With *determinate* sentencing practices, those who are convicted and sentenced to prison receive a set time—a number of years. With an *indeterminate* sentencing model, those who are convicted must generally prove that they are behaviorally ready to return to society. Alexander Maconochie first promoted the practice: "sentences should not be for imprisonment for a period of time, but for the performance to be determined and specified quantity of labour; in brief, time sentences should be abolished, and task sentences substituted" (Barry, 1956, p. 151).

Maconochie furthers a powerful proposition: *task* specific sentencing practices.

In theory (if not practice), indeterminate sentencing practices remove the power of release from the courts and give the power to correctional institutions. These models also build in incentives for good behavior—a man or woman in prison can "earn" time back, can "earn" an earlier release. And it leads us to this important question:

> Do you think that prison sentences should be for a set number of years or should we consider other factors when determining a sentence?

Obviously, time does not necessarily indicate behavioral change. But keep in mind, if we move beyond time-specific sentences then we also appear to be asking corrections to substantially alter internal operations—opportunity for "tasks," for "behavioral" change must be readily available. And this question cannot be asked outside of the conditions we place upon it: the existence of the prison institution is *not challenged*; and since its conception, the prison itself has not been widely challenged as an institution (with rare exceptions).

> The US fully accepts the prison as an institution; would we accept it in the same way if our unrelenting goal was public safety?

Regardless, the fixes offered at the end of 19th century *assumed the necessary existence* of prison—without formal discussion. Most scholars refer to the era between the 1890s and the 1930s as the Progressive era. The term rehabilitation did not officially appear as a focus in correctional institutions until the 1930s. But the emphasis at the end of the 19th century and the beginning of the 20th century certainly focused on restoring the individual who had quarreled with the law by targeting work and providing job training.

From the 1930s until the 1970s, the focus was formally on rehabilitation with two models gaining wide adoption:

Medical Model (1930s–1960s)

Community Model (1960s–1970s)

The medical model treated those who offended as "sick" in need of individualized treatment. Suitably, this approach targets individual differences, emphasizes offender classification, ostensibly studies root causes of criminal participation. The prison comes to rely on trained professionals–*psychiatrists*–to diagnose, treat, counsel, even "shock!"

The focus of the community model–a model that may become far more relevant in the coming years–targets reintegration, educational, and vocational training. This model avoids incarceration when possible, prioritizes probation (community supervision).

But we largely abandoned rehabilitation by the mid-1970s.

Review Chapter 6 for a detailed explanation as to why rehabilitation fell out of favor. But consider here the following: if rehabilitation is no longer a reasonable goal of punishment–and we still care about future criminal participation by currently punished individuals–then we are left with deterrence and incapacitation (since retribution demands no change in future behavior).

It is clear that we did not abandon the prison in the 1970s. Instead, we came to rely much more on imprisonment. We dramatically increased the size of the incarcerated population in the last three decades of the 20th century–we increased it *seven fold!* Yes, seven times as many people were incarcerated by the first decade of the 21st century as were incarcerated just 30 years earlier. And without rehabilitation as a formal goal, we warehoused (incapacitated) millions of men and women and hoped to instill fear in the process (deterrence).

Indeed, by the late 20th century, corrections was about managing populations instead of managing individuals. Sentencing policy was largely concerned with increasing time served–truth in sentencing laws, habitual offender laws, three strike penalties–and increasing prison admissions (e.g., the drug war).

But none of this was inevitable. Remember: the colonists did not actively consider prison as a solution to crime because it would've been illogical: why feed and house an individual who has violated the rules of the colony? Why remove the labor, the needed contribution, and make a child out of an adult?

These questions are not designed to push you in a particular direction but to question the institutions that we currently govern. We spend close to $80,000,000,000 on corrections each year in the United States. Estimates of our state of Connecticut suggest that in 2015 we spent just over $1000,000,000 on incarceration alone to incarcerate fewer than 16,500 people (Vera Institute of Justice, 2015).

Consider the following two data points:

> 95% of those incarcerated will return home
>
> About 650,000 people return home every year

Now consider the hypothetical case:

> John spends 15 years in prison for armed robbery. John serves his sentence, holds himself responsible by our own state standards, and is released.

While in prison, John was told:

> When to wake up
>
> When to eat
>
> When to report to work
>
> When he could use the facilities
>
> When he could visit commissary
>
> When he could report to the visiting area to see his family
>
> > How to embrace his mother
> >
> > How to play with his child
> >
> > How to dress
> >
> > > *It is also likely during the 15 year imprisonment John was threatened, scared, violent, and so on*

For 15 years, John has been told what he can and cannot do; he has been granted no autonomy over those decisions and is afforded no chance to develop independent life skills. When he is released after 15 years, do you believe he will be more like a functioning adult or more like a child?

Why would we create a nanny state of punishment in the United States?

RETHINKING THE ROLE OF PRISON

John's case above demonstrates the trouble with limiting autonomous living for those who are actively involved in the process of reentering society. It might be necessary for some severely antisocial men and women to be confined in such a restrictive manner (even for extended periods). But what should the transition look like? How should the state address the needs of the individual—who in all likelihood will be released—and provide the necessary support so that the same individual is able to live independently, work, pay taxes, *contribute.* Indeed, an indeterminate sentencing model allows for outcomes beyond time to dictate release. But it also requires that a more flexible understanding of prison is probably necessary. Most people get out. If we want to reduce the likelihood of re-offending—and lessen the severe impact of institutionalization—we might need to change the manner in which we supervise. This would require us to improve the bonds between those in prison and those who provide emotional (and maybe even financial support) in the community. This would also require us to make sure those who leave are "employment-ready"—have the skills (interpersonal, vocational, social) to adapt to the work environment. And it probably makes sense for us to slowly reintroduce men and women to the outside world.

But these are all solutions at the *back-end*, or *after prison*. Are we doing enough at the *front-end*, or before prison? Diverting men and women away from prison *toward* treatment programs is important. But what if we invested more in *why* the contact with the system in the first place?

This leads us to abolition. This might seem like a sudden transition. And by discussing abolition we are not necessarily endorsing it. But considering abolition of prison is important because it simply allows us to imagine a world without prison and imagine what that world would require.

There is a certain hysteria around even suggesting abolition—*what would you do with all those really terrible violent people!*—a refrain that is often skewed toward the most dangerous of people and overlooks the general nature of crime and of punishment. But there is a much more important point: abolition is about the future, about setting in motion conditions that make prisons unnecessary, useless, futile.

If prison were no longer an option, we would be forced to address the conditions that increase the likelihood of criminal participation and we would be forced to address hot spots of incarceration. In terms of imprisonment, we do not pull equally across states, across cities, across towns.

Where you live matters. And hotspots of incarceration are also hotspots of disadvantage.

Let us not confuse the issue: the question is not about proving or disproving the utility of prison; the question is what is the best way to reduce *crime—future* crime (those who will participate in criminal acts for the first time in the future and those who will participate in criminal acts *again* in the future). If we become too consumed by whether or not prison is able to deter or rehabilitate or incapacitate we are also too consumed with the requirement of the institution.

Putting people in prison *because prison exists* is not a solution; putting people in prison because we have logically and empirically found that prison—forced confinement—is a requirement for certain populations *might* be a solution. But even this latter point would be deemed insufficient by abolitionists because with prison we essentially allow ourselves to be lazy in fighting crime; we are not fighting the known predictors of criminal participation.

As we see it, abolitionists would like us all to begin with one simple question: should we be able to predict with reasonable accuracy the likelihood of criminal participation based on geographical location, race, and/or class? Do we believe that social structures—regardless of biological composition—are sufficient at providing prosocial support and insulating individuals from crime? This is the central point of abolitionists: imprisonment comes to the already harmed and there is a mountain of evidence supporting the allegation that hurt people are more likely to hurt others.

If prison were no longer an option, abolitionists argue, we would be *forced* to acknowledge the known predictors of criminal participation—complications that often appear very early in life. Abolition is not about releasing dangerous people in society; abolition is about preventing those people from *becoming* dangerous and using all the resources at our disposal to target prevention. If you were to adopt this perspective, what kinds of responses to crime would emerge?

Can we imagine a world without prison? The colonists largely couldn't imagine a world with prison.

CHAPTER 9

CHILDREN AND JUSTICE

> America is now home to thickening ranks of juvenile "superpredators"—radically impulsive, brutally remorseless youngsters, including ever more preteenage boys, who murder, assault, rape, rob, burglarize, deal deadly drugs, join gun-toting gangs and create serious communal disorders. They do not fear the stigma of arrest, the pains of imprisonment, or the pangs of conscience (Bennett, DiIulio, & Walters, 1996, p. 27).

This chapter deals with justice system responses to the behavior of children. The preceding quote comes from the text *Body Count: Moral Poverty and how to win America's War Against Drugs*. The book was published in 1996 and informed us about a "new type" of child—the "juvenile superpredator"—who was fundamentally different from existing children. It warned us of the havoc they would wreak and that little could be done to prevent it. The idea of the juvenile superpredator caught the imagination of politicians and the general public; it reshaped reactions to crime by children. Fear over the juvenile superpredator led to passage of legislation designed to protect us from this "new breed": some jurisdictions passed laws eroding the traditional confidentiality of children's proceedings and making information from them available to schools and to other social agencies; some states passed laws increasing the number of acts for which juveniles are automatically tried as adults; other states made it difficult to have children's records expunged *after* reaching adulthood; other jurisdictions began allowing juvenile records to be submitted as evidence in criminal court (Kappeler & Potter, 2005). Reaction to the juvenile superpredator is a great example of how mass media contribute to our thoughts about crime and our reactions to crime. Importantly, the authors of *Body Count* were wrong. The work has been widely condemned: Berkley Law Professor Franklin E. Zimring has stated that the "theories on superpredators were utter madness" (Becker, 2001). We raise this issue at the beginning of the chapter because it is the image of the fictitious juvenile superpredator our students seem to gravitate toward when asked to think about crime by children. Widely publicized atrocities seem to suggest to many that the juvenile superpredator is real: he is not. It is true that children do commit atrocious acts and we should be outraged by them; but to approach the topic of children's justice with such atrocities as exemplars of children's crime is entirely misleading. Data published by the *Office of Juvenile Justice and Delinquency Prevention* provide context here: in 2017 child arrests for murder and nonnegligent manslaughter composed only 0.42% of all juvenile arrests for index crimes (Office of Juvenile Justice and Delinquency Prevention, 2018).

Before continuing, we must discuss the importance of language. In this chapter, we refer to underage people as "children"; any other term obscures what we are discussing (though referencing children is not typically part of the formal language of "juvenile justice"). We know no one who recounts achievements of their "juvenile" or how proud they are of their "youth" or "adolescent." People speak about their child, their children, their sons, their daughters. Referring to children more accurately reflects that we are dealing with vulnerable people who have not developed to meet societal standards for "adulthood"; while we recognize stages in childhood are delineated by language ("adolescent" or "preteen") reference to children avoids making our subject abstract and keeps front and center what we are dealing with. We are also concerned that referring to the "juvenile" rather than the "child" implies an underlying difference between the two. Rather than referring to "delinquents," "juvenile justice," or the "juvenile justice system" we refer to "children who offend," "children's justice," and "the children's justice system." While this means you will not learn the formal language of "juvenile justice" we believe our approach is important to avoid the subject matter seeming abstract; doing so encourages you to remember we are discussing children and to reflect upon language effects in the field of crime and justice. We encourage you to question and reject existing language, when appropriate, regardless of its popularity.

THE STATUS OF CHILDREN

In shaping our responses to crime by children, we must think about what we mean when referring to children. Today children and adults are treated differently in the criminal justice system; there are separate children's courts, procedures, and facilities. At first glance, this different response seems natural: children and adults are clearly different. But there is nothing natural about how the justice system responds to children's behavior. Examination of justice system responses to children reveals considerable variation over time and location. We examine how our justice system responds to the behavior of children and begin by examining why adults and children are treated differently.

At first glance it may seem that as with adults, children who offend threaten the social contract so their *actions* should be punished accordingly. If we focus on actions it is clear the girl and the woman can cause equal harm: the girl's actions could be *even* more harmful. So why respond differently to the behavior of children? It is only when we recognize children as developing individuals who have not yet acquired the necessary "stuff" to be held fully responsible for their behavior that we understand the necessity of different justice system responses to their behavior. What is the "stuff" children are lacking? It is generally recognized that children under a certain age lack the ability to intentionally engage in criminal activity and this has resulted in the "infancy defense" to crime; exactly what children are lacking that justifies the infancy defense is controversial and has varied over time (Cipriani, 2009), but there is some agreement that children do not act with a full understanding of the consequences of their actions.

Different responses to the behavior of children and adults are not inevitable and are not without controversy. Recent years have seen changes in justice system responses to children that *do* focus on behavior rather than characteristics of actors; for example, there has been an increase in the number of offenses for which children can be tried as adults (Bernstein, 2014). We hear the slogan "adult time for adult crimes" (Frontline, 2014), which speaks to this issue. But take a moment and think about this slogan; what does it really mean? We do not understand it. What is an adult crime? What is adult time? A separate children's justice system has already been established affirming our recognition of meaningful differences between children and adults. But such slogans *do* highlight the importance of our reactions: just as there is nothing inevitable about treating children differently from adults there is also nothing inevitable about treating them the same as adults. We acknowledge some behaviors are so egregious we may want to treat all actors the same, react only to actions, but we do not *have* to do this. We can also see that there are many behaviors for which children can be treated like adults based only on their actions and without real consideration of their age or circumstances. For example, children in different jurisdictions can be tried as adults for a variety of offenses including drug possession and public order crimes (Bernstein, 2014).

As with adults, it is important to ask what it is we want to achieve through our response to illicit behavior by children. From its inception the goal of justice system responses to the behavior of children has been rehabilitation; we respond to those children who participate in illicit acts by assuming that they need help; in doing so we hope they will avoid offending in the future. Acknowledging the goal of rehabilitation is important as this is an issue that can be examined empirically—through research we can determine whether our responses to unacceptable behavior by children reduce the likelihood of recurrence. As with adults we must remember that the vast majority of children return to our communities; above all our reactions to their offensive behavior must decrease the chance of repeat behavior.

So why respond differently to the behavior of children?

Let's consider Plato's perspective:

> No creature is ever born in possession of that reason, or that amount of reason, which properly belongs to it when fully developed; consequently, every creature, during the period when it is still lacking in its proper intelligence, continues all in a frenzy, crying out wildly, and, as soon as it can get on its feet, leaping wildly (Chambliss, 1979, p. 99).

Plato recognized children are not fully developed; recognition of the need for different responses to the behavior of children has long existed. But while the development of children is natural, acknowledging the *importance of* development in our *reactions to* children is not. Attitudes toward children reflect historical processes and reveal nothing natural about our reactions to their behavior. For example, history reveals infanticide to have been common practice at different times (Kilday, 2013; Rotar & Teodorescu, 2011). Historically, incarcerating children with adults has been common *and continues today* (Bernstein, 2014). Throughout history, art reveals visual depictions of children as "little adults," dressed in smaller versions of adult clothing (Ariès, 1962).

While immaturity and development may be natural characteristics of childhood, it is important to examine why we came to recognize these differences and how they led to separate justice system reactions to behavior by children. Understanding this process emphasizes different treatment of children is the product of decisions, not nature, and as such, radical change is possible any time.

DISCOVERING CHILDHOOD

During the 19th century, the emergence of "Houses of Refuge" reflect now familiar concerns over the treatment of children in the justice system; these concerns and subsequent changes in the treatment of children are often referred to as "the discovery of childhood" (Frijhoff, 2012). Prior to the Houses of Refuge, while the developmental nature of childhood may have been recognized, it did not always translate into how children were treated; they were often incarcerated in facilities with adults where they experienced significant abuses (Krisberg & Austin, 1978). The Houses of Refuge became the first rehabilitation facilities designed for children, recognizing their vulnerability and reflecting the belief that there is a shared social obligation to care for them:

> These prisons should be rather schools for instruction, than places of punishment, like our present State Prisons where the young and the old are confined indiscriminately. The youth confined there should be placed under a course of discipline, severe and unchanging, but alike calculated to subdue and conciliate. A system should be adopted that would provide a mental and moral regimen (Krisberg & Austin, 1978, p. 15).

While they may not have lived up to their benevolent aspirations, Houses of Refuge marked the beginning of a *change in how we react* to children involved in illicit activity. This culminated in 1899 with the first separate children's court. While there is disagreement over the motives of those involved in establishing the Houses of Refuge (Platt, 1974), the emergence of these institutions were important because of their stated rehabilitative purpose and far-reaching effects. An important legal concept in the continuing development of institutions for children and the first children's court is *parens patriae*. Taken from legal practices in England, *parens patriae* translates to "parent of the country" (Levesque, 2011) indicating that ultimately the state has an obligation to ensure the well-being of children. In an 1838 case, *Ex Parte Crouse*, a father contested the right of the county of Philadelphia to place his daughter in a House of Refuge at her mother's request *when she had committed no crime*. The ruling in this case is particularly important because it clearly defined what was to become the rationale underlying development of the children's justice system:

> The object of the charity is reformation, by training its inmates to industry; by imbuing their minds with principles of morality and religion; by furnishing them with means to make a living; and, above all, by separating them from the corrupting influence of improper associates. To this end may not the natural parents, when unequal to the task of education, or unworthy of it, be superseded by the *parens patriae*, or common guardian of the community? ... The infant has been snatched from a course which must have ended in confirmed depravity; and not only is the restraint of her person lawful, but it would be an act of extreme cruelty to release her from it (Mennel, 1972, p. 75).

Here, we see establishment of the paternalistic intent of the children's justice system; when parents were seen as unfit or unable to control their children, the state would assume their role.

It is important to highlight an assumption being made in adopting *parens patriae*. The court ruling states "(t)he infant has been snatched from a course which must have ended in confirmed depravity." What does this mean? Clearly, the court is stating that a life of depravity was certain for this specific child if action was not taken. To put it another way, the court was making a prediction—if we don't intervene the outcome is certain. This raises an important question: to what extent can we really be confident in predictions we make about the future of *individual* behavior? If you think of your own childhood experiences, how accurately might someone have predicted outcomes for you *as an individual adult* based upon your childhood experiences and actions?

The first court established exclusively to deal with children was in Cook County, Illinois, in 1899, and embraced *parens patriae*; recognizing the developmental nature of childhood, the court developed distinctive policies and practices. The court aimed to keep children out of secure facilities and probation officers were employed to investigate the background of children brought to the court, make recommendations to the court on how to treat them, and supervise children following court action (Tuthill, 2001). This court, and its approach to children, marked the beginning of the modern children's justice system: children are completely separated from adults; children are dealt with in a separate system employing specialized language and practices; and the state recognizes the developmental nature of childhood.

So how do we operationalize childhood in the justice system? We do this through age and laws recognizing deficits of youth are not new; in England during the Middle Ages, for example, 7 years came to indicate the beginning of legal responsibility (Corriero, 2006).

But using age to determine what constitutes childhood is problematic; decisions regarding age-appropriate behavior show the difficulty of using age to establish childhood. Across states there is disagreement about what the age of adulthood should be; and this has changed over time and location: For example:

> Alastair aged 16 years and 11 months lives in a state where everyone under 17 is legally a child. He runs away from home and is arrested for it. He can be processed through the children's justice system and may even be incarcerated.

> Douglas aged 17 years lives in the same state. He runs away from home but is not subject to intervention by the justice system for his behavior.

There are more significant consequences of using age as a cutoff point for distinguishing children from adults:

> Robert is 15 years and 10 months. He lives in a state where everyone under 16 is a child and cannot be incarcerated beyond age 21. He is found guilty of murder, incarcerated, and released when he turns 21.
>
> Keith is 15 years and 10 months. He lives in a state where anyone over age 14 can be tried as an adult for a violent offense. He is accused of murder, found guilty, and sentenced to 25 years in prison.

Age is a proxy for an essential missing "thing" or "things" not obtained until a certain level of maturity. But what does age represent? Legally, age is used to determine the point at which people are judged to be fully responsible for their behavior and so subject to the full criminal justice system. But there are clearly problems in using age to make this distinction because we do not all possess the same attributes at a given age. Anecdotally, we are sure you can think of people who are "immature" or who fail to meet the expected behavioral standards of their chronological age. But what precisely does this mean? Empirical evidence indicates important behavioral abilities develop across childhood and into adulthood; we do not possess the same abilities at the same time and do not possess some important abilities (e.g., impulse control) until well into adulthood (Monahan, Steinberg, & Piquero, 2015; Shulman, Harden, Chein, & Steinberg, 2015). Age alone fails to recognize these important developments. A "one-size-fits-all" strategy where everyone under a certain age is treated as children while those over it (perhaps by only a few days or hours) is problematic. As we illustrate below, there is increasing court recognition, incorporating empirical evidence, that age alone is problematic for distinguishing between children and adults in the justice system.

THE U.S. SUPREME COURT AND CHILDREN

Recognition of essential differences between children and adults concerning criminal responsibility are reflected in U.S. Supreme Court decisions. And these decisions show that the treatment of children has been subject to great change. Capital punishment is one issue showing how attitudes can change over a short period of time and how evidence concerning child development is incorporated into dealing with children. In *Thompson v. Oklahoma* (1988), the Supreme Court established that no one can be executed for offenses committed prior to their 16th birthday. In *Stanford v. Kentucky* (1989), the U.S. Supreme Court considered whether children aged 16 or 17 years at the time they committed a capital crime could be executed. In its majority opinion, the 1989 court ruled that children aged 16 and 17 years *could* be executed under certain circumstances. In its ruling the court recognized that the use of age in *determining the legality of most behaviors does not represent an indivualized assessment of maturity for each accused child*, but that such individualized assessment is required in capital cases:

> There is no relevance to the state laws cited by petitioners which set 18 or more as the legal age for engaging in various activities, ranging from driving to drinking alcoholic beverages to voting. Those laws operate in gross, and do not conduct individualized maturity tests for each driver, drinker, or voter; an age appropriate in the vast majority of cases must therefore be selected. In the realm of capital punishment, however, individualized consideration is a constitutional requirement. (*Stanford v. Kentucky*, 1989, p. 374–377)

So, in 1989, the U.S. Supreme Court established that no one can be executed for acts prior to their 16th birthday but that 16- and 17-year olds can be executed. The court's ruling in *Stanford v. Kentucky* raised a number of questions, including, if individual consideration is needed in dealing with children accused of capital crimes, why is such individual consideration not necessary for other behavior?

In 2005, capital punishment was again considered by the U.S. Supreme Court in *Roper v. Simmons*. In this instance, the court explicitly recognized the developmental nature of childhood and in its opinion stated:

> The susceptibility of juveniles to immature and irresponsible behavior means "their irresponsible conduct is not as morally reprehensible as that of an adult." ... Their own vulnerability and comparative lack of control over their immediate surroundings mean juveniles have a greater claim than adults to be forgiven for failing to escape negative influences in their whole environment ... The reality that juveniles still struggle to define their identity means it is less supportable to conclude that even a heinous crime committed by a juvenile is evidence of irretrievably depraved character. From a moral standpoint it would be misguided to equate the failings of a minor with those of an adult, for a greater possibility exists that a minor's character deficiencies will be reformed. Indeed, "[t]he relevance of youth as a mitigating factor derives from the fact that the signature qualities of youth are transient; as individuals mature, the impetuousness and recklessness that may dominate in younger years can subside." ... ("For most teens, [risky or antisocial] behaviors are fleeting; they cease with maturity as individual identity becomes settled ...") (*Roper v. Simmons*, 2005, p. 570).

Further recognition of the difference between juveniles and adults came in 2010 with the Supreme Court ruling in *Graham v. Florida*. The issue at stake here was whether juveniles could be incarcerated for life without the possibility of parole for *nonhomicide* offenses. In this ruling, the court reiterated the differences between children and adults highlighted in *Simmons*, stating (in part):

> Here one cannot dispute that this defendant posed an immediate risk ... Graham deserved to be separated from society for some time in order to prevent what the trial

> court described as an "escalating pattern of criminal conduct," ... but it does not follow that he would be a risk to society for the rest of his life. Even if the State's judgment that Graham was incorrigible were later corroborated by prison misbehavior or failure to mature, the sentence was still disproportionate because that judgment was made at the outset. A life without parole sentence improperly denies the juvenile offender a chance to demonstrate growth and maturity (*Graham v. Florida*, 2010, p. 73).
>
> *Note: as we discuss above the* ***U.S. Supreme Court*** *here is acknowledging that we are really bad at predicting future individual behavior from past behavior even if it may seem reasonable to do so.*

In *Miller v. Alabama* (2012), the Supreme Court considered whether children convicted of murder could be sentenced to life without the possibility of parole. Again recognition of the difference between juveniles and adults is emphasized in extending the standard set in *Roper v. Simmons* and *Graham v. Florida* to children convicted of murder. In its ruling in *Miller v. Alabama*, the court specifically cites its rationale pertaining to decisions in *Roper v. Simmons* and *Graham v. Florida*, stating (again, in part): "(o)ur decisions rested not only on common sense–on what 'any parent knows'–but on science and social science as well" (2012, p. 8) and continued "Roper and Graham emphasized that the distinctive attributes of youth diminish the penological justifications for imposing the harshest sentences on juvenile offenders, even when they commit terrible crimes" (2012, p. 9). The court further stated:

> To recap: Mandatory life without parole for a juvenile precludes consideration of his chronological age and its hallmark features–among them, immaturity, impetuosity, and failure to appreciate risks and consequences. It prevents taking into account the family and home environment that surrounds him–and from which he

> cannot usually extricate himself—no matter how brutal or dysfunctional. It neglects the circumstances of the homicide offense, including the extent of his participation in the conduct and the way familial and peer pressures may have affected him (2012, p. 477).

The opinion notably concludes with: "the Eighth Amendment forbids a sentencing scheme that mandates life in prison without possibility of parole for juvenile offenders" (2012, p. 479).

It is clear from these cases that what constitutes childhood is complex and *subject to change*. Clearly, chronological age is not enough; the U.S. Supreme Court asserted that an individualized approach *is necessary* in capital cases; this highlights that—in general—children were not being treated as individuals but rather as "types" that fit unjustified preconceptions and unjustified predictions about individual behavior. These preconceptions crucially overlooked the vital elements that shape behavior (namely, individual experience and physical development). As the Supreme Court noted in *Miller v. Alabama* it is not appropriate to judge children solely on their actions because they are significantly more susceptible to environmental influence than adults.

Given the Supreme Court's position is it appropriate to continue treating children as adults for some behaviors? Should a record of *childhood* misbehavior be allowed to influence how someone is treated as an adult?

STATUS OFFENSES

Status offenses comprise an important difference in justice system responses to the behavior of children. Unlike adults, children can be punished for behavior that is *only wrong because of their status as children*. Status offenses include things like running away from home (see example above), incorrigibility, possession of alcohol or tobacco, habitual truancy, and habitual refusal to follow the orders of a parent or guardian (Smoot, 2014). It may seem "natural," especially following *parens patriae*, that the state has the right to intervene when children display problematic behavior. However, one of the challenges with status offenses is that they can lead children to contact with the justice system for behaviors that are part of typical adolescent rebellious behavior. Recognizing that typical adolescent behavior should not lead children to involvement in the justice system, Congress passed the *Juvenile Justice and Delinquency Prevention Act* in 1974. This act called for the development of diversionary programs to keep status offenders out of the justice system. While there has been success in reducing the number of status offenses referred to children's court, almost 95,000 cases were referred in 2016; the majority of these referrals were for truancy (57%), alcohol violation (12%), ungovernability (9%), runaway (8%), and miscellaneous transgressions (8%) (Hockenberry & Puzzanchera, 2018, p. 64). There are a number of concerns here. With truancy, for example, it seems unlikely that referring a child to court will increase his or her desire to return to school. Furthermore, what is "ungovernability"? What does this actually mean? Ungovernability is so vague as to capture all manner of behaviors. A major challenge with status offenses is their vague definition: the people involved in making decisions about whether behavior qualifies as a status offense and what should be done about it have a degree of discretion that has been found to contribute to bias and inconsistency within the children's justice system:

> Whether or not misbehavior lands a kid in court is largely dependent on the individuals who respond to the behavior and how they view the kid who is "acting out." Be it a police officer, a school official, or even a parent, adults have varying levels of knowledge around youth development and particular ideas about what acceptable family and social norms look like. These understandings converge with their personal biases (including racial, cultural, and gender biases) to shape how they interpret and respond to a kid's misbehavior (Jafarian & Ananthakrishnan, 2017).

Historically, girls have suffered more punishment for status offenses than boys: girls were more likely to be sent to secure institutions than boys and they continue to be referred to the children's justice system more often than boys for minor status offenses (Jafarian & Ananthakrishnan, 2017). More recently the status offense category has been identified as significant in the emergence of the "school-to-prison pipeline."

SCHOOL-TO-PRISON PIPELINE

The school-to-prison pipeline refers to an established link between schools and the children's justice system: rather than helping children avoid involvement in the justice system it is known that for many, the school experience actually *increases* their likelihood of justice system involvement. Historically little relationship between school and the justice system existed, the relationship is not inevitable; a *change in reaction* to student behavior created the school-to-prison pipeline. During the 1980s, schools became less tolerant and began thinking of once typical and routine student misconduct (e.g., tardiness, disrespect) as problems requiring official action. As a result, the number of out-of-school suspensions increased rapidly (Tyner, 2017). Children suspended from school are at risk for more involvement in status offenses and their behavior subject to closer scrutiny once returning to school leading to additional sanctions. At the same time, as schools became less tolerant of misbehavior, there was an increase in the presence of police in schools (SROs, or School Resource Officers). With police in school, behavior once dealt with informally by teachers was increasingly referred to police with the result that the number of police referrals to court greatly increased. There is strong evidence that out-of-school suspensions and contact with the children's justice system greatly increase the likelihood of school failure, involvement in delinquency, and ultimately more contact with the justice system and justice officials (Jafarian & Ananthakrishnan, 2017; Mallett, 2015).

The school-to-prison pipeline also exemplifies the tremendously tragic level of racial bias throughout the criminal justice system including the children's justice system: disproportionate minority contact is found at each stage of the children's justice system with minority children more likely to be processed through it (Mallett, 2015). However, data reveal a staggering level of disproportionate minority contact as part of the school-to-prison pipeline:

> Since 1975, African American students have been suspended from school at two to three times the rates of Caucasian students ... Nationwide, African American students constitute 18% of students but represent 39% of expulsions and 42% of referrals to law enforcement while in school, and in more disparate contrast, African American and Hispanic students constitute 42% of students but account for 72% of those arrested for school-related offenses (Mallett, 2015, p. 573).

While it is beyond the scope of this volume to more fully discuss the problem of disproportionate minority contact with the justice system for children, we believe evidence from the school-to-prison pipeline helps illustrate the extent of the problem. It is important to reiterate that a significant proportion of acts leading children into the justice system by way of school are acts that would have traditionally been dealt with in school by teachers (Nolan, 2011).

Most offenders first engage in crime as children, so how we react to their behavior is important. But how we react to children is not inevitable; it is influenced by many factors. We hope to have illustrated that defining childhood is complicated, subject to change, and that the definition has significant consequences for children's lives. We also hope our consideration of status offenses and the school-to-prison pipeline illustrates how our decisions have led children engaged in relatively typical childhood behavior to be involved with the justice system.

How would you define childhood and what are the implications of your definition for justice system intervention? What behaviors do you think should warrant intervention by the justice system? What form do you think justice system intervention in the lives of children should take?

CHAPTER 10

SHAPING OUR JUSTICE FUTURE

The following comes from the podcast *Serial* (season 3, episode 5). Host Sarah Koenig discusses what she took from an interview with Brian Radigan, a prosecutor in Cleveland, Ohio:

> ... And when he's thinking about sentences, it was also striking to learn what Brian was not thinking about—deterring crime ... He doesn't come to work every day thinking about criminal justice policy. That's not what's guiding him.

Brian Radigan is quoted as stating:

> You know deterrence, and laws, and how to fix communities, and all that type of stuff—I try not to think of it that way. I think it's just we're better off worrying about our victims here. Because when I'm talking to somebody that had their son killed, or their daughter killed, or mother raped and murdered, they don't care about the deterrent. They don't give a shit about somebody else's kid, or whatever, they care about what am I doing for them. And that's how I try to keep it ...
>
> ... I don't know that we deter people. We hope we do. I mean, that's why we have some of these sentences and things like that. But we've got gun specs now for people that, if you commit a crime with a gun, you're going away for more prison ... but I don't know if it's eliminated the amount of guns that are on the streets (Koenig, 2018).

For those working in the justice system, many of the issues we address in this text lack obvious relevance; not because people don't think about them or do not care, but because when working in the justice system priorities change. Justice professionals enter an environment where their focus must be on day-to-day activities; they perform their work as best they can according to existing expectations. Prosecutors like Brian Radigan may not really consider justice; instead prosecutors focus on how to move cases rapidly through an overburdened system and how to give crime victims what they think is needed. Correctional officers may really care about the well-being of those they supervise; but their focus is most likely on avoiding injury and returning safely home at the end of a shift. And police may consider law *enforcement* to be the only real policing function. Because these professionals all operate in an environment with already established goals, traditions, and values, it is perhaps unreasonable to expect those currently working in the justice system to fashion meaningful change in it.

But prosecutors like Brian Radigan are still making choices and those choices are embedded in the existing retributive ideal. Many prosecutors believe their role is to satisfy the needs of the victims; but we should not simply assume that prosecutors are actually satisfying the victim. Absent clear evidence—not anecdotal commentary—that decisions are actively improving the *lives* of victims and the *lives* of all who are victimized within her jurisdiction, the claims of prosecutors are largely unimpressive. Does the prosecutor actually make the community safer? What is the prosecutor's responsibility to public safety?

We know crime is emotional—people are harmed; we know crime is intimate—people who are victimized often take it personally. Reflexive responses *seem* to be rational, sensible, and effective. It is, perhaps, reasonable for many to shout: "*We should hit back!*" But if we adopt and endorse a retributive system, then we cannot make claims that the other goals of punishment are also met *along the way*. We need evidence that the goals of punishment—those goals that look at future criminal participation—are indeed met. We must ask:

> Are we safer?
>
> If we are safer is it because of policies our justice agencies have adopted?
>
> If we are safer can justice agencies prove it is because of their policies that we are now safer?

Why is this entire discussion so important? Because if we subscribe primarily to retributive policies it is possible that we are doing so *instead of* alternative policies. Many prosecutors seem only casually concerned about deterrence—nothing in their actions strives to meet the demands of deterrence. And many prosecutors appear to have little concern for rehabilitation.

> Is this what the public wants?
>
> Is this what the public believes they deserve?
>
> Does the public even know the work of prosecutors is not typically empirically supported or guided by clearly defined goals?

We believe that justice agencies need to clearly define their goals and the public needs to formally approve those goals. If the goal of the justice system is to "hit back"—and the public formally acknowledges this as the goal—then prosecutors adopting this approach are at least working to satisfy citizen wishes. However, if the goal of the system is to make the streets *safer*—to prevent and reduce criminal participation—then many prosecutors are not adequately serving the people in their community. If prosecutors are unable to present evidence as to how they are making their jurisdiction safer—what specific policies they are adopting, what evidence they are using to adopt such policies—then they are evading their responsibility as a public official. Prosecutors like Brian Radigan have a responsibility to the entire community not only those immediately impacted by crime events. To emphasize this point, if our neighbor were robbed we would want to know that our justice agencies were doing everything possible to ensure we also were not robbed at some later date.

Data do not always tell the story we think they will tell. For example, it often seems to be "common sense" that prison must deter future criminal participation; it is "common sense" until we look at recidivism rates. Once we begin to look at data, we see our assumptions about behavior are often misguided. The data often tell us that we might have to allocate resources differently. But there are two embedded issues in Criminal Justice practice: one is philosophical (what we want the system to do) and the other is empirical (how should the system demonstrate that it is indeed accomplishing what it purports to be accomplishing). What we come to know through science—through empirical evidence—should change what we do; but *why* we do what we do is reflective of who we are and what we want out of our society.

What type of protection do we want from and by the government?

Keep in mind: new approaches are always needed. We constantly need to improve practices. And remember: Criminal Justice practice and policy has evolved dramatically over the past 200 years. The world today is not like the world was in 1830 when police first appeared across cities in the Northeast. The problems of today are *different* than the problems in 1830 or 1930—should our justice agencies adapt to those differences?

Consider the following questions:

Should police demonstrate that they make the community safer?

Should police demonstrate that they prevent criminal participation?

Should corrections agencies prove that they reduce future criminal involvement?

Should prosecutors prove—as public officials—that they are making the community safer?

Even though we believe that the answer to each of the above questions is "yes"—we are not asking you to agree. Instead, we are asking you to agree with our *process*. Logically stating the intention of the agency and asking for evidence that the intention is met. It is important to note that demonstrating effectiveness of justice practices is an *ongoing* process—our justice agencies must continually and rigorously reevaluate what they do. Context, location, and time all matter. What works in Baltimore might not work in Boston; what works in one neighborhood in Chicago might not work in another; what worked in the 1950s might not work in 2019. But the approach, the *process* to uncover, assess, and reassess what actually works, is the same. Prosecutors may claim they are serving the interests of victims—but ask yourself the following:

> Do we actually know what victims want or might we act on assumptions stemming from our own perspective?

We do not deny that people do terrible things to each other. But we ask how do we develop a system that recognizes the needs of actual victims *and* makes the community safer, stronger, better? While we focus mainly on prosecutors here the same process should be applied to examining the actions of other justice system professionals.

This text is designed to help readers remember that justice institutions are not inevitable; justice institutions, ideally, are developed and continue developing in *response* to public needs. Said differently, if crime is our central concern then our central task is to reduce and eliminate crime in the most effective manner. Our proposal asks you, in part, to consider what types of institutions would be part of an empirically based solution to crime.

If we begin to think in terms of what we want our justice system to achieve, then we are able to pursue ideas that may alter the justice landscape. We might *change* what we expect from police (we might even fundamentally alter the institution). We might *change* how we use prison. We might *change* how we respond to the criminal behavior of drug-addicted men and women. But change is not a requirement; we are not demanding a baseless reorganization of justice agencies; instead, we are asking the institutions to prove that what they do is what we want them to do and if not, acquire empirical evidence to help them change accordingly. But remember, we can hardly expect current practitioners to give these questions serious consideration (even though many will sincerely try to) because they must operate within their existing environment.

Ultimately, crime is a social construct—we decide what constitutes crime. We live in an active world—rules are made by us, defended by us. This is because it is our social world. We cannot decide the laws of nature nor do we decide our genetic composition (at least not yet). But we can decide, as a collective, what our rules should be and what the punishment should be for violating those rules. But this is never complete; the world 200 years ago would cause most of us great trouble if we fell into it—*even though it is the past.* Colonists would likely be equally (if not more) disoriented if they were to magically enter our world.

Therefore, we should be informed by—*but not controlled by*—the past. Constant change within the social system calls for a continual revisit of our institutions and requires that we challenge those institutions to defend their necessary role in our current social state. For example, it is true that we have prisons; we may even need prisons to some extent; but do we need to incarcerate a greater proportion of our population (and especially the vulnerable) than any other country in the world? Our use of prison should prompt you to ask questions: does this make us safer? Is there *evidence* that our imprisonment rate makes us safer?

We have proposed—directly and indirectly—that our justice institutions should be able to clearly:

1. State their purpose
2. Evaluate their effectiveness at meeting that purpose

So what would it take to make it possible for these institutions to evaluate their effectiveness at meeting their stated purpose? What should be the purpose of police? Of corrections?

> *Why should we have a justice system and how do we ensure that it represents and protects all of us?*

It just might make sense to agree on what we *need* and *want* and then ask our institutions to meet those needs and wants.

REFERENCES

Affordable Housing Online. (2019). *Criminal record requirements for HUD housing programs*. Salisbury, MD: Affordable Housing Online. Retrieved from https://affordablehousingonline.com/guide/criminal-records-housing/hud-requirements

Alper, M., Durose, M. R., & Markman, J. (2018). 2018 Update on prisoner recidivism: A 9-year follow-up period (2005–2014). *NCJ, 250975*, 1–23.

Altimari, D., & Poitras, C. (2007). Parole an issue after Cheshire slayings. Hartford, CT. *The Hartford Courant*. Retrieved from https://www.courant.com/community/hc-petit0727-story.html

Ambrose, S. A., Bridges, M. W., DiPietro, M., Lovett, M. C., & Norman, M. K. (2010). *How learning works: Seven research-based principles for smart teaching*. Hoboken, NJ: John Wiley & Sons, Incorporated.

Anderson, E. (1999). *Code of the street: Decency, violence, and the moral life of the inner city*. New York, NY: W.W Norton.

Ariès, P. (1962). *Centuries of childhood: A social history of family life*. New York, NY: Knopf.

Avery, B., & Hernandez, P. (2018). *Ban the box: US cities, counties and states adopt fair hiring policies*. New York, NY: National Employment Law Project. Retrieved from https://www.nelp.org/publication/ban-the-box-fair-chance-hiring-state-and-local-guide/

Barry, J. V. (1956). Pioneers in criminology. XII. Alexander Maconochie (1787–1860). *The Journal of Criminal Law, Criminology, and Police Science, 47*, 145–161.

Barthe, E. P., Leone, M. C., & Lateano, T. A. (2013). Commercializing success: The impact of popular media on the career decisions and perceptual accuracy of criminal justice students. *Teaching in Higher Education, 18*, 13–26.

Beccaria, C. (1764). Of crimes and punishments. In J. E. Jacoby, T. A. Severance, & A. S. Bruce (Eds.), *Classics of criminology* (4th ed., pp. 406–419). Long Grove, IL: Waveland Press Inc.

Becker, E. (2001). As ex-theorist on young "superpredators," bush aide has regrets. *The New York Times*. Retrieved from https://www.nytimes.com/2001/02/09/us/as-ex-theorist-on-young-superpredators-bush-aide-has-regrets.html

Becker, H. S. (1963). *Outsiders; studies in the sociology of deviance*. London, England: Free Press of Glencoe.

Bennett, W., DiIulio, J., & Walters, J. (1996). *Body count: Moral poverty and how to win America's war against crime and drugs*. New York, NY: Simon & Schuster.

Berger, A. A. (2005). *Media analysis techniques*. Thousand Oaks, CA: Sage.

Bernstein, N. (2014). *Burning down the house: The end of Juvenile prison*. New York, NY: The New Press.

Blackburn, P. (2018). *Super bowl 2018 commercials: Here's how you can watch these leaked TV ads*. Retrieved from https://www.cbssports.com/nfl/news/super-bowl-2018-commercials-heres-how-you-can-watch-these-leaked-tv-ads/

Bohm, R. M. (1986). Crime, criminal and crime control policy myths. *Justice Quarterly, 3*, 193–214.

Braithwaite, J. (1996, March). Restorative justice and a better future (Crime, punishment and the criminal justice system). *The Dalhousie Review,* pp. 9–31.

Braithwaite, J. (2002). *Restorative justice and responsive regulation*. Cary, NC: Oxford University Press, Incorporated.

Callanan, V. J. (2005). *Feeding the fear of crime: Crime-related media and support for three strikes*. New York, NY: LFB Scholarly Publishing LLC.

Calvert, C., & Torres, M. (2011). Putting the shock value in first amendment jurisprudence: When freedom for the citizen-journalist watchdog trumps the right of informational privacy on the internet. *Vanderbilt Journal of Entertainment and Technology Law, 13*, 323.

Carli, S. (2015). The love affair between philosophy and poetry: Aristotle's poetics and narrative identity. *The Southern Journal of Philosophy, 53*, 151–177.

Cavender, G., & Bond-Maupin, L. (1993). Fear and loathing on reality television: An analysis of "America's most wanted" and "Unsolved mysteries". *Sociological Inquiry, 63*, 305–317.

Center for Justice and Reconciliation. (2019). *RJ in the criminal justice system*. Washington, DC: Center for Justice and Reconciliation. Retrieved from http://restorativejustice.org/restorative-justice/rj-in-the-criminal-justice-system/#sthash.PAEiKljN.dpbs

Chambliss, J. J. (1979). Human development in Plato and Rousseau: "Training from childhood in goodness". *The Journal of Educational Thought (JET)/Revue De La Pensée Éducative, 13*, 96–108.

Chomsky, N. (1997). What makes mainstream media mainstream. *Z Magazine*. Retrieved from https://chomsky.info/199710__/

Christie, N. (1977). Conflicts as property. *The British Journal of Criminology, 17*, 1–15.

Cipriani, D. (2009). *Children's rights and the minimum age of criminal responsibility: A global perspective*. Abingdon, England: Routledge.

Clear, T. R. (2012). Response 3: The big society in the context of a changing justice system. *Criminology & Criminal Justice, 12*, 500–505.

Corriero, M. A. (2006). *Judging children as children: A proposal for a juvenile justice system.* Philadelphia, PA: Temple University Press.

Cox, J. W., & Rich, S. (2018). No, there haven't been 18 school shootings in 2018. That number is flat wrong. Washington, DC. *The Washington Post.* Retrieved from https://www.washingtonpost.com/local/no-there-havent-been-18-school-shooting-in-2018-that-number-is-flat-wrong/2018/02/15/65b6cf72-1264-11e8-8ea1-c1d91fcec3fe_story.html?utm_term=.3bf1ec82a7d6

Cullen, F. T., & Gilbert, K. E. (1982). *Reaffirming rehabilitation.* Cincinnati, OH: Anderson Pub. Co.

Cullen, F. T., & Gilbert, K. E. (2013). *Reaffirming rehabilitation; the 30th anniversary edition.* New York, NY: Taylor and Francis.

Cullen, F. T., & Jonson, C. L. (2011). Rehabilitation and treatment programs. In J. Q. Wilson & J. Petersilia (Eds.), *Crime and public policy* (chap. 11, pp. 293–344). New York, NY: Oxford University Press. In J. Q. Wilson & J. Petersilia (Eds.), *Crime and public policy* (pp. 293–344). New York, NY: Oxford University Press.

DiIulio, J. J., Jr. (1991). Understanding prisons: The new old penology. *Law and Social Inquiry, 16*, 65–99.

Federal Bureau of Investigation. (2018). Crime in the United States 2017. *United States Department of Justice*. Retrieved from https://ucr.fbi.gov/crime-in-the-u.s/2017/crime-in-the-u.s.-2017

Fishman, M. (1978). Crime waves as ideology. *Social Problems, 25*, 531–543.

Fishman, M., & Cavender, G. (1998). *Entertaining crime: Television reality programs.* New York, NY: Aldine de Gruyter.

Freud, S. (1961[1930]). *Civilization and its discontents*. New York, NY: Norton.

Friedman, L. (1993). *Crime and punishment in American history*. New York, NY: Basic Books.

Frijhoff, W. (2012). Historian's discovery of childhood. *Paedagogica Historica, 48*, 11–29.

Frontline. (2014). Juvenile justice: From both sides. *Public Broadcasting Service (PBS)*. Retrieved from https://www.pbs.org/wgbh/pages/frontline/shows/juvenile/bench/adulttime.html

Gilliam, F. D., & Iyengar, S. (2000). Prime suspects: The influence of local television news on the viewing public. *American Journal of Political Science, 44*, 560–573.

Graham v. Florida, 560 U.S. 48, 73 (2010).

Gramlich, J. (2016). *Voters' perceptions of crime continue to conflict with reality*. Washington, DC: Pew Research Center. Retrieved from http://www.pewresearch.org/fact-tank/2016/11/16/voters-perceptions-of-crime-continue-to-conflict-with-reality/

Griffin, T., & Miller, M. K. (2008). Child abduction, AMBER alert, and crime control theater. *Criminal Justice Review, 33*, 159–176.

Gun Violence Archive. (2018). *Mass shootings*. Retrieved from http://www.shootingtracker.com/

Harding, R. (2014). Rehabilitation and prison social climate: Do 'what works' rehabilitation programs work better in prisons that have a positive social climate? *Australian & New Zealand Journal of Criminology, 47*, 163–175.

Hartnagel, T. F., & Templeton, L. J. (2012). Emotions about crime and attitudes to punishment. *Punishment & Society, 14*, 452–474.

Heffernan, W. C. (2017). Addressing issues of justice (and injustice) in criminal justice education. *Journal of Criminal Justice Education, 28*, 112–128.

Herman, E., & Chomsky, N. (2002). *Manufacturing consent; the political economy of mass media*. New York, NY: Pantheon Books.

Hockenberry, S., & Puzzanchera, C. (2018). *Juvenile court statistics 2016*. Pittsburgh, PA: The National Center for Juvenile Justice. Retrieved from https://www.ojjdp.gov/ojstatbb/njcda/pdf/jcs2016.pdf

Hoffman, D. (2017). *The economic impact of prison rehabilitation programs*. Philadelphia, PA: University of Pennsylvania. Retrieved from https://publicpolicy.wharton.upenn.edu/live/news/2059-the-economic-impact-of-prison-rehabilitation/for-students/blog/news.php

Hurley, D. C., & Hurley, M. H. (2015). Education alone is not the answer: The Specter of right-wing authoritarianism for criminal justice majors at three institutions. *Journal of Criminal Justice Education, 26*, 371–389.

Illescas, S. R., & Frerich, N. (2014). Crime and justice reinvestment in Europe: Possibilities and challenges. *Victims & Offenders, 9*, 13–49.

Jafarian, M., & Ananthakrishnan, V. (2017). *Just kids: When misbehaving is a crime*. New York, NY: Vera Institute of Justice. Retrieved from https://www.vera.org/when-misbehaving-is-a-crime#introduction

Johnson, D. (2009). Anger about crime and support for punitive criminal justice policies. *Punishment & Society, 11*, 51–66.

Kappeler, V. E., & Potter, G. W. (2005). *The Mythology of Crime and Criminal Justice*. Long Grove, IL: Waveland Press.

Karstedt, S. (2002). Emotions and criminal justice. *Theoretical Criminology, 6*, 299.

Kelling, G. L., Pate, T., Dieckman, D., & Brown, C. (1974). *The Kansas City preventative patrol experiment: A summary report, 1974*. Washington, DC: Police Foundation.

Kilday, A. -M. (2013). *A history of infanticide in Britain, C. 1600 to the present*. London, England: Palgrave Macmillan Limited.

Koenig, S. (2018). *Serial: Season 3*. Chicago, IL: This American Life. Retrieved from https://serialpodcast.org/season-three/5/transcript

Krisberg, B., & Austin, J. (1978). *The children of Ishmael: Critical perspectives on Juvenile justice*. Palo Alto, CA: Mayfield.

Lambert, E. G. (2005). Worlds apart: The views on crime and punishment among white and minority college students. *Criminal Justice Studies, 18*, 99–121.

Lemert, E. (1951). Primary and secondary deviation. In J. E. Jacoby, T. A. Severance, & A. S. Bruce (Eds.), *Classics of Criminology, Fourth Edition* (pp. 351–353). Long Grove, IL: Waveland Press Inc.

Levesque, R. (2011). Parens patriae. *Encyclopedia of Adolescence, 4*, 1962–1964.

Lippmann, W. (1930). *Public opinion*. New York, NY: Macmillan.

Liska, A. E., Lawrence, J. J., & Sanchirico, A. (1982). Fear of crime as a social fact. *Social Forces, 60*, 760–770.

MacKenzie, D. L. (2006). *What works in corrections: Reducing the criminal activities of offenders and delinquents*. Cambridge, England: Cambridge University Press.

Mallett, C. A. (2015). *The school-to-prison pipeline: A comprehensive assessment*. New York, NY: Springer Publishing Company.

Martinson, R. (1974, Spring). What works? Questions and answers about prison reform. *The Public Interest, 35*, 22–54.

McCarthy, J. (2016). Americans' views shift on toughness of justice system. *Gallup*. Retrieved from https://news.gallup.com/poll/196568/americans-views-shift-toughness-justice-system.aspx

McChesney, R. W. (2004). *The problem of the media: U.S. communication politics in the twenty-first century*. New York, NY: Monthly Review Press.

McGuinn, S. C. (2018). *Reentry, desistance, and the responsibility of the state: Let them back in*. United Kingdom: Emerald Publishing. ProQuest Ebooks

McGuinn, S. (2014). *Prison management, prison workers, and prison theory: Alienation and power*. Lanham, MD: Lexington Books.

Mennel, R. M. (1972). Origins of the juvenile court: Changing perspectives on the legal rights of juvenile delinquents. In T. C. Calhoun & C. L. Chapple (Eds.), *Readings in Juvenile Delinquency and Juvenile Justice* (pp. 72–81). Upper Saddle River, NJ: Prentice Hall.

Merton, R. K. (1948). The self-fulfilling prophecy. *The Antioch Review, 8*, 193–210.

Miller v. Alabama, 567 U.S. 460, 477 (2012).

Miller v. Alabama, 567 U.S. 460, 479 (2012).

Monahan, K., Steinberg, L., & Piquero, A. R. (2015). Juvenile justice policy and practice: A developmental perspective. *Crime and Justice, 44*, 577–619.

Moons, W. G., & Mackie, D. M. (2007). Thinking straight while seeing red: The influence of anger on information processing. *Personality and Social Psychology Bulletin, 33*, 706–720.

Munves, J., & Kelner, J. (2016). *The Kent State coverup*. Newburyport, MA: Open Road Distribution.

National Reentry Resource Center. (2019). *About the National Inventory of Collateral Consequences of Conviction*. Washington, DC: US Department of Justice. Retrieved from https://niccc.csgjusticecenter.org/about/

Newburn, T. (2005). Symbolic politics and penal populism: The long shadow of Willie Horton. *Crime, Media, Culture, 1*, 72.

Nickerson, R. S. (1998). Confirmation bias: A ubiquitous phenomenon in many guises. *Review of General Psychology, 2*, 175–220.

Nixon, R. M. (1971). *Remarks about an intensified program for drug abuse prevention and control*. University of California, Santa Barbara, CA: The American Presidency Project, UC Santa Barbara. Retrieved from https://www.presidency.ucsb.edu/documents/remarks-about-intensified-program-for-drug-abuse-prevention-and-control#axzz1PCJydjl5

Nixon, R. M., United States. President (1969–1974: Nixon) and United States. Office of the Federal Register. (1971). *Public papers of the Presidents of the United States, Richard Nixon: Containing the public messages, speeches, and statements of the president, 1969 to August 9, 1974*. Washington, DC: U.S. G.P.O.

Nolan, K. (2011). *Police in the hallways: Discipline in an urban high school*. Minneapolis, MN: University of Minnesota Press.

Office of Juvenile Justice and Delinquency Prevention. (2018). *OJJDP statistical briefing book*. Washington, DC: Bureau of Justice Statistics. Retrieved from https://www.ojjdp.gov/ojstatbb/crime/qa05101.asp?qaDate=2017

Orwell, G. (1949). *1984*. London, England: Secker and Warburg.

Palmer, T. (1975). Martinson revisited. *The Journal of Research in Crime and Delinquency, 12*, 133.

Paternoster, R. (2010). How much do we really know about criminal deterrence? *The Journal of Criminal Law and Criminology (1973), 100*, 765–824.

Pettit, B. (2012). *Invisible men: Mass incarceration and the myth of black progress*. New York, NY: Russell Sage Foundation.

Pinard, M. (2010). Collateral consequences of criminal convictions: Confronting issues of race and dignity. *New York University Law Review, 85*, 457–534.

Pinker, S. (2013). *Decivilization in the 1960s*. University of Michigan: Michigan Publishing. Retrieved from https://quod.lib.umich.edu/h/humfig/11217607.0002.206/--decivilization-in-the-1960s?rgn=main;view=fulltext

Platt, A. (1974). The child-saving movement and the origins of the Juvenile justice system. In P. M. Sharp & B. W. Hancock (Eds.), *Juvenile delinquency: Historical, theoretical, and societal reactions to youth* (pp. 3–18). Upper Saddle River, NJ: Prentice Hall.

Potter, G. W., & V. E. Kappeler, (Eds.). (2006). *Constructing crime: Perspectives on making news and social problems*. Prospect Heights, IL: Waveland Press.

President's Commission on Law Enforcement and the Administration of Justice. (1967). *The Challenge of crime in a free society*. Washington, DC: United States Government Printing Office.

Quinney, R. (1970). *The social reality of crime*. Boston, MA: Little, Brown.

Rogers, E. M. (2003). *Diffusion of innovations* (5th ed.). New York. NY: Free Press.

Roper v. Simmons, 543 U.S. 551, 570 (2005).

Rotar, M., & Teodorescu, A. (Eds.). (2011). *Dying and death in 18th-21st century Europe*. Newcastle-upon-Tyne, England: Cambridge Scholars Publishing.

Rothman, D. J. (1995). Perfecting the prison. In N. Morris & D. J. Rothman (Eds.), *The Oxford history of the prison* (pp. 100–116). New York, NY: Oxford University Press.

Rousseau, J. -J. (2005[1762]). *The social contract*. New York, NY: Barnes and Noble.

Sampson, R. J., & Loeffler, C. (2010). Punishment's place: The local concentration of mass incarceration. *Daedalus, 139*, 20–31.

Sever, B., & Grillo, M. (2016). Do our books reinforce criminal justice stereotypes? An analysis of the images in introductory criminal justice textbooks. *Journal of Criminal Justice Education, 27*, 53–75.

Shelden, R. G., Brown, W. B., Miller, K. S., & Fritzler, R. B. (2016). *Crime and criminal justice in American society* (2nd ed.). Long Grove, IL: Waveland Press.

Shulman, E. P., Harden, K. P., Chein, J. M., & Steinberg, L. (2015). Sex differences in the developmental trajectories of impulse control and sensation-seeking from early adolescence to early adulthood. *Journal of Youth and Adolescence, 44*, 1–17.

Smoot, N. (2014). *Status offenses: A national survey*. Washington, DC: Coalition for Juvenile Justice. Retrieved from http://www.juvjustice.org/sites/default/files/resource-files/Status%20Offenses%20-%20A%20National%20Survey%20-FINAL%20-%20WEB.pdf

Stanford v. Kentucky, 492 U.S. 361, 374–377 (1989).

State of Connecticut Judicial Branch. (2017). *Accelerated rehabilitation*. Retrieved from https://www.jud.ct.gov/Publications/CR137D.pdf

Stuntz, W. J. (2011). *The collapse of American criminal justice*. Cambridge, MA: Harvard University Press.

Surette, R. (2014). *Media, crime, and criminal justice: Images, realities and policies* (5th ed.). Belmont, CA: Cenage Learning.

Swift, A. (2016). Americans' perceptions of U.S. crime problems are steady. *Gallup*. Retrieved from https://news.gallup.com/poll/197318/americans-perceptions-crime-problem-steady.aspx

The Division on the Study of American Fears. (2018). *The chapman survey of American fears*. Orange, CA: The Earl Babbie Research Center. Retrieved from https://www.chapman.edu/wilkinson/research-centers/babbie-center/survey-american-fears.aspx

The Scottish Government. (2016). *National Strategy for Community Justice*. (pp. 1–52) Edinburgh, Scotland: The Scottish Government.

Thomas, B. (2015). *Narrative: The basics*. London, England and New York, NY: Routledge, Taylor & Francis Group. ProQuest Ebooks.

Thomas, W. I., & Thomas, D. S. (1928). *The child in America: Behavior problems and programs*. New York, NY: Alfred A. Knofp.

Thompson v. Oklahoma, 487 U.S. 815 (1988).

Tomkovick, C., Yelkur, R., & Christians, L. (2001). The USA's biggest marketing event keeps getting bigger: An in-depth look at super bowl advertising in the 1990s. *Journal of Marketing Communications, 7*, 89–108.

Tuthill, R. S. (2001[1899]). The Juvenile court law in cook county Illinois, 1899. In T. C. Calhoun & C. L. Chapple (Eds.), *Readings in Juvenile delinquency and Juvenile justice* (pp. 59–62). Upper Saddle River, NJ: Prentice Hall.

Tyner, A. R. (2017). The emergence of the school-to-prison pipeline. Washington, DC: American Bar Association. Retrieved from https://www.americanbar.org/groups/gpsolo/publications/gpsolo_ereport/2014/june_2014/the_emergence_of_the_school-to-prison_pipeline/

Van Wormer, K. S., Walker, L., & SAGE Publications. (2013). *Restorative justice today: Practical applications*. Los Angeles, CA: SAGE.

Vera Institute of Justice. (2015). *The price of prisons: Prison spending in 2015*. New York, NY: Vera Institute of Justice. Retrieved from https://www.vera.org/publications/price-of-prisons-2015-state-spending-trends/price-of-prisons-2015-state-spending-trends/price-of-prisons-2015-state-spending-trends-prison-spending

Vollmer, A. (1933). Police progress in the past twenty-five years. *American Institute of Criminal Law and Criminology, 24*, 161.

Wacquant, L. (2010). Class, race & hyperincarceration in revanchist America. *Daedalus, 139*, 74–90.

Wagner, P., & Rabuy, B. (2017). *Following the money of mass incarceration*. Northampton, MA: Prison Policy Initiative. Retrieved from https://www.prisonpolicy.org/reports/money.html

Wales, K. (2001). *A dictionary of stylistics*. Harlow, England and New York, NY: Longman.

Walker, S. (2015). *Sense and nonsense about crime, drugs, and communities*. Stamford, CT: Cengage.

Wilson, J. Q., & Kelling, G. L. (1982). Broken windows. *Atlantic Monthly, 249*(3), 29–38.

Wimshurst, K., Marchetti, E., & Allard, T. (2004). Attitudes of criminal justice students to australian indigenous people: Does higher education influence student perceptions? *Journal of Criminal Justice Education, 15*, 327–350.

Zehr, H. (1985). Retributive justice, restorative justice. *New Perspectives on Crime and Justice, 4*, 1–19.

CPSIA information can be obtained
at www.ICGtesting.com
Printed in the USA
LVHW060736260819
628601LV00002B/1/P

9 781524 977276